# THE ASPIRING MILLIONAIRE

## By Bill Bailey

Copyright 1988 by

**ASPIRING MILLIONAIRES PUBLISHING HOUSE**

Sacramento, CA

Cover concept, illustration, total graphic production of book, and partial photography by: **Rick Spears**, Sacramento,CA ▾ (916) 973-8181

Computer Phototype by : **Spears Graphics Express**, Seattle, Wash.

Additional Photography (unless noted) by : **Bill & Dorie Bailey.**

First Printing 1988
Printed in the United States of America

Library of Congress Catalog ing in Publication Data 87-71995

ISBN 0-9618781-0-X

## WARNING — DISCLAIMER

This book has been written and designed only to provide non-specific information intended for educational purposes regarding subject matter.

It is available to the public with the understanding the publisher and author are not engaged in rendering legal, accounting, or other professional services. Investments exhibited or suggestions offered are not to be taken or considered without first consulting the appropriate professional who can more specifically evaluate your particular situation.

The Aspiring Millionaire is not a get-rich scheme, nor does it promise any positive results. The ideas and academic suggestions are all based on extensive interviews by successful millionaires who most all agree that it takes hard work and persistence to achieve financial success.

This book is meant for reference use only. It contains information on financial matters that might not fit your circumstances and information which can easily become outdated. For this reason we suggest you review any suggestions offered with a qualified professional.

The purpose of this book is merely to offer some stimulating ideas and educate the reader in the particular subject matter.

The author and publisher shall be neither liable or responsible to any person or entity regarding any loss or damages said to be directly or indirectly caused or alleged to be caused by the subject matter or information contained in the book.

# TABLE OF CONTENTS

# PART III. THE BASICS:
# WHAT YOU NEED TO KNOW ABOUT MONEY

## TABLE OF CONTENTS

Throughout this book, the word "he" is used when referring to the individual in the grammatical singular. No disrespect, chauvinism, or attitude of inequality is felt or intended. Ease of statement is. Eventually our language will replace the awkward constructions of he/she, s/he, his or her with a fluid, unclumsy, undifferentiating pronoun to confirm that the individual—male or female—is valuable and significant.

I dedicate this book to the millions of individuals who have wondered what opportunities are available to enhance their financial strengths; who have feared economic dependency upon others; and who have crossed into the dimension of positive attitudes and creativity. I salute those who are ambitious—yet prudent, eager, shrewd; those who have been willing to sacrifice today's pleasures for tomorrow's success; those who have taken control of their lives and not given up and fallen prey to self-defeat; those who do not fear hard work, planning, and sacrifice. You have paid your dues several times over. You will soon be considered the wealthy who have all the breaks.

# ACKNOWLEDGMENTS

I would like to thank the people who have helped me with the development of my career and this book.

Thanks to Ed for directing me into the field of financial planning, Al for exposing me to the basics of developing a financial practice, and Roger for spending the time necessary for me to master the specifics of financial planning. I would also like to thank Whitney and Ann who both, as college interns, assisted in the development of this book. Both are now fully involved in finance careers of their own and are very successful.

A final and special thanks to the International Association of Financial Planners for developing a very valuable training organization for practicing financial planning, and to my wonderful clients who so graciously maintained our professional relationship and continually refer others.

# PREFACE

My birth name is Hunter William Bailey. I was born in 1953 to a father who had served in or worked for the U.S. Armed Forces for most of his life. In his day, financial security was something attained only by staying employed by the government for 30 years and retiring at a salary slightly higher than that necessary for survival. In the last year of my father's working life, he spoke of retirement with great pleasure and pride; after all these years he could come and go as he pleased, never having to be somewhere on time, never having to account for his actions. That last year, Mr. Kenneth Abraham Bailey died.

Other life experiences influenced my attitude about financial independence. My mother, Madalyn, was 40 years old at my birth. A young woman during the depression, she knew the difficulties of financial life, and she constantly reminded me what life could be like for the average person during hard times. In the depression, Americans were out of work, did not eat regularly, and lost their pride. Life was tough, and no one wasted anything, nor did they take things for granted. A person was lucky if he had a job and more fortunate to be able to feed his family. Surviving a brother and father, I learned that life is not always fair and is only what I can make of it. Why work long hours doing something I didn't enjoy? Why wait my whole life for the day I could do what I wanted to do? I therefore set out to live a life with freedom from financial dependence and freedom to set and achieve goals that would leave me with a feeling of self-gratification.

After graduating from college with a degree in pre-law, I soon realized that the legal profession did not always provide the personal and financial independence I desired. I decided to join the county sheriff's reserve-deputy program and at the same time build a financial estate. In the first five years of this plan, I worked part-time as a reserve deputy for reasonable pay and completed training and educational programs in the fields of investment brokerage and financial planning. I worked seven days a week at an hourly rate as a jailer dealing with life on the negative side as I trained with professionals with great aspirations and success stories in the field of finance. I soon developed the extra bankroll and experience needed to set out and begin my own investment advisory practice. I even purchased my first office building in which to house my practice.

I enjoy the sport of making money and creating financial independence. I feel that every dollar made takes me further away from the poverty roll and allows me to live the lifestyle I desire and the time and money to help others through charitable and rehabilitative organizations. I wish the same freedom for everyone.

# INTRODUCTION
## TO HAVE OR NOT TO HAVE: THAT IS THE QUESTION

- Have you ever imagined what it would be like to be financially successful?

- Are you looking for answers that will take you from your current situation and utilize your available resources to assure a profitable direction?

- How would you feel if you could look at your checkbook and see several thousand dollars; if you could review your investment accounts and have the cash to buy the car of your choice or a trip to any place in the world, to have total financial and emotional freedom from money worries, to know that whether the economy remains stable or experiences the ravages of inflation you will have control of your financial destiny?

If your first answers to these questions are resounding nods of enthusiasm, you are headed in the right direction. By imagining and wondering, you have taken the first step in beginning a serious commitment toward improving your present financial situation and learning that wealth for you and your family is available through various means.

This book is designed to help you realize the reality of financial independence and ease. It is not a formula or "gimmick" book. It will not show you how to become a millionaire in six easy steps. It does not even promise that all who read it will be fantastically wealthy. Rather, it is a common-sense approach to financial planning. The theme of the book is using common sense to develop a coherent, comprehensive, and workable financial plan and then developing the self-discipline to stick to it.

For example, there are many life techniques to master in order to begin accumulating a fortune:

1. *Be eager; have the drive to get ahead.*

2. Just as a business would gear up for more profitable times, *cut your losses and reduce unnecessary spending habits.* Do things as cheaply as possible.

3. *Be consistent; take it seriously; think about your financial future.* No one else will. In nature, creatures that do not fend for themselves will not survive; those that cannot live out a cold winter must plan. The eager beaver builds a home out of twigs and branches. Each twig is placed very carefully to help create

the sum total of his winter home. Each dollar you save is like another twig in a wall that stands with great strength, weathering any storm.

4. *Always remember that every dollar is created equally and they all spend the same.* Let your money work for you. When you spend a dollar, ask yourself, "Do I really need this item? Will it improve my financial position? Will it be there when I need it? Or will it have been lost to some temporary, self-gratifying whim?" If invested, those dollars can be put to work seven days a week even while you sleep.

5. *THINK, THINK, THINK about what you are doing.* Before making any major financial decisions, stop and analyze your alternatives. Picture what you are about to do, and do some homework. Seek professional advice unless you are well versed and experienced enough to really know what you are doing. Never move on a hunch or hot tip. Good deals are hard to come by, so beware of "the great deal." Chances are if it's too good to be true, then it's too good to be true.

6. *Plan for the worst, yet enjoy the best.*

All the above is not to say that money is the most important thing in life. However, to live the good life and to prevent your some day being a burden on others, self-sufficiency is a desirable goal. And should you overshoot your targeted financial needs, there are always tax-deductible, charitable gifts that can be made to the benefit of others.

Beyond reminding you about common sense, this book provides information about resources available so you can clarify exactly what types of strategies fit your needs. You will learn about risk factors and the advantages of time. You will be exposed to basic do's and don't's and have various technical information on hand that is made easy to understand and is quickly referenced. This is a bottom-line financial manual that should be kept by your side and referred back to in order to upgrade your skills and improve your spirits.

This book will in . . .

**Part I.** guide you through the process—a step-by-step "how-to";
**Part II.** introduce you to basic concepts of money, money management, and the acquisition of wealth;
**Part III.** present the specifics of insurance, taxes, and investments.
Overall, this book will assist you in making informed choices about how to begin and how to continue on your journey to the status of millionaire.

# INTRODUCTION

The process of achieving financial independence will not be easy initially; it will take hard work and sacrifice. All the cliches still apply: "You cannot get something for nothing." "There is no such thing as a free lunch." "Money doesn't grow on trees." "No pain, no gain." But if you work hard, plan, and save now, you can relax and enjoy later.

So, are you ready for the ride of your life? Is this going to be just another good book where the author has some great ideas but you just can't seem to take your first step? Or is this going to be that first commitment that leads to your dream come true?

## PART I
# THE PROCESS

*Only those few who are willing to try
will obtain their dreams*

Dr. Paula Dwelly. A professional family counselor in her own business

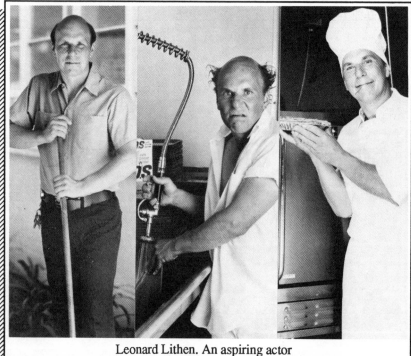

Leonard Lithen. An aspiring actor

# STEP 1:

# DREAM THE DREAM

Life is what we imagine it to be. We can imagine ourselves eagles soaring high in the sky looking for a camouflaged morsel, then swooping down and swiftly striking at opportunity before it escapes. Or we can imagine ourselves a white knight prevailing against the dragon, staring the dragon in the face, doing battle and protecting our kingdom from those who would take it away.

More specifically, we can imagine having income from investments and businesses which run themselves. We receive a salary and dividend checks simply because we planned and made good decisions; our company or small business sends us a monthly check from the profits of our earlier hard work as we shop and spend money all day or sit on a beach in Jamaica.

The key is that we imagine. We dream. In our fantasies, we see ourselves in a given life pattern behaving in a given way. Sometimes we mix and match our self-visions; sometimes all our imaginings focus to one goal, one way of being. In the process of dreaming our dreams, we begin to form the reality of our lives.

And so, Step 1 in the dream of achieving financial independence is just that:

## DREAM THE DREAM

The more specifically you can define the dream the more concrete will be your goals. Let the images filter through—the more the better. Take time with your fantasies so they become clearer and clearer. Ask yourself questions:

1. How do I see myself—my clothes, my home, my lifestyle— in five years? In ten years? In twenty years?

2. How do I want to spend my time twenty years down the road?

3. What activities—sports, travel, wine-making—do I want to engage in five years from now? Ten years? Twenty?

4. Where do I want to live? What style of house? Surrounded by whom?

5. What surroundings do I want for my children? What style of life when they turn ten? Fifteen? Twenty?

6. How do I want to walk, laugh, move during my "golden years," and when do I want those golden years to begin?

As the dream materializes in all its glorious specifics, your confidence and energy will surge. You will begin to feel like an eagle, a knight, a person with potential and power.

And, having dreamed the dream, you will be ready to take on THE WORLD.

# STEP 2:

# DEFINE THE DREAM

Your head is full of rich and glorious fantasy. Your vital signs are charged. You want to take off and do.

Well, as with any journey you decide to take, you need a road map. To chart *your* road map on *your* journey to "Aspiring Millionaire," you need to synthesize the dreams you have dreamed into specific goals— your destinations.

These goals can be anything—from being a millionaire by the time you're 35 to establishing a trust fund for your grandchildren—but make them specific.

I want *(to create an estate, net worth of $1,000,000)* by the time I'm *(35)* in order to *(insure the safety of my family's well being).*

I want *(to retire with an income of $2,500 net each month)* by the time I'm *(45)* in order to *(work full-time on writing the Great American Novel).*

The goals need to be reality based. To leap from a $25,000 salary, no-asset position at age 34 to $1,000,000 in the bank at age 35 is not reasonable; to accomplish the task by age 40 is, however, within the realm of possibility.

After you have set your goals, break them into smaller portions or objectives. Set a time table to meet each objective. Then reduce your goals to a specific set of actions to be taken monthly, weekly, or even daily.

And the goals need not be colossal. In fact, a good technique for clearing the decks before starting out on the longer journey is to set short-term goals: pay up unpaid bills, complete incompleted projects and other tasks that are bothering you at the present. Instead of complicating things with new tasks and ideas, go back and clear your conscience. You will need a clear and sound foundation from which to start.

As you define the dream, begin disciplining yourself to stick to your objectives. You will discover that as you accomplish each "little" objective, the goals will begin to take care of themselves. To quote an old cliché, "Genius is 10% inspiration and 90% perspiration."

Work hard toward your goals, and time will take care of the rest.

You may have to work at two jobs, work six or seven days a week. You may have to tighten your belt and cut back on spending in order to get extra cash to invest. But in the long run, your sacrifices will pay off. Even if you don't become extremely wealthy, you will at least have enough for a comfortable retirement.

The road you take on your adventure to "Aspiring Millionaire" will not be without sudden curves and unexpected bumps. But if you hold on to the road map of your dream and never give up, no matter how low you might feel—or how old—your ride to success will be a thrilling journey on the ups and downs of the Road to Prosperity. As each new turn curves in unexpected angles, you can regroup your thoughts, review your plans, and charge forward, following your fantasies until they become a reality. At first, you may brake in awe at the tremendous length of the road, be intimidated by its scary ups and downs and windy turns and great slopes. But once you begin the ascent to the top and glance over your shoulder to reflect on the exciting miles you have traveled, you will wonder about having hesitated to take the ride. Those very ups and downs and sharp curves make the journey rich in experience and fulfillment.

So buckle your seat belt and hang on. You are about to begin a new life!

But first:

# STEP 3:
# SHAPE THE DREAM

Have you ever stopped to think about the qualities that many foreigners who come to this country and create fortunes possess? Where did they acquire the money to purchase real estate, establish businesses, and create financial independence?

I use foreigners as an example only because they are very obvious to us. We don't tend to notice the American down the street who becomes rich because he or she has always been there, but when people from other countries begin to work hard and take financial risks and succeed, we begin to notice.

We need to understand what qualities these people have. What is it that makes them work harder, band together in large family organizations, form small communities, and end up controlling financial interests in many areas of the U.S.? If we stop to think, we realize these foreigners are much like our own distant relatives who came to this country with a dream. Our relatives also banded together as a large family and worked together, protecting each other and becoming the forefathers of this great country. We can learn from those who have left poverty and come to America to become millionaires. How did they do it?

There are various techniques; yet, more importantly, personal attitudes must be acquired in order to achieve personal financial success. Regardless of your starting point in life, the most important vehicle for financial success is your attitude toward reaching your goals. How committed are you? The answer to this question will determine your financial future.

It is true that you might inherit thousands of dollars, receive a court settlement from an unfortunate damage to you or a family member, become that one-in-a-million entertainer or actor who experiences stardom, or even hit it big in the lottery or at the race track. What are your chances of any one of these fantasies occurring?

The true secret to financial success is utilizing the raw materials around you to produce a sustaining and enriched financial future. To do that, you need to:

## Step 3:1:
## Recognize the Obstacles That Stand in Your Way

There are many different attitudes about self and money. Some people know nothing but hard work as a base for venturing out to discover what they can do. Others are cynical and reject every good idea of financial advancement. Some people just do not have the knowledge of what, where, when, and how to get started on the path of financial independence. Many believe they are prisoners of a low-income society much like a prisoner in a jail cell.

A few people will take the initiative and unlock the cell door with the key of positive attitudes. They realize all is not easy and not every attempt will succeed, yet they try—and then try again. For it is not the cell walls and bars that hold us prisoner; it is the idea—and fear—that we cannot open the door and walk through it that keeps us from trying. The longer we wait, the rustier that door is going to become and the harder to open, for whether the door is locked or unlocked is solely determined by our attitudes.

## THE OUTCAST SYNDROME

It has been said, "Poor is popular." In many cases where classes of people work 40 hours a week just to survive, a certain comraderie develops, a comraderie centered in a somewhat pessimistic attitude and a subsequent ridicule of the desire to get ahead.

You may be surrounded by individuals who choose not to strive for the better life—or fear they can't or believe they haven't the right—and when you do, you feel like an outcast. This attitude and fear can make or break you.

I soon realized this concept in my early years of law enforcement. To supplement my business income, I worked as a deputy sheriff in my home town on a part-time basis. One of the first statements of people in custody was, "There ain't no opportunities." They seemed to crave group sympathy for their present situation. Their society as a whole re-enforced the fact that they did not have a chance at life, yet they never once expressed the desire to learn what opportunities lay just blocks away from the jail. They lacked the desire to seek out and learn to change their lives because they felt a comraderie with their friends and fellow prisoners. If they did desire something more than what everyone else had, they feared they would be outcast from the group for being different.

Banishment—being an outcast—someone who no longer has anything in common with old friends and familiar lifestyles—is one of our biggest fears. If you are "rich," you have something other people do not have. You are different now.

# SHAPE THE DREAM

In the early stages of your financial plan for success, friends and family will give you a hard time for not living your life as they would; your penny pinching, working seven days a week, and making sacrifices will become a source of discussion for them; you are apart from them. Not long ago when I began my dream of wealth and missed or was late to family functions, I was questioned about my lifestyle and advised not to work so hard. Family and friends disagreed with my aspirations and reminded me that there are other things in life than making money. Well, I had to agree with them in part—yes, there are other things in life. However, I knew that life's pleasures don't just happen. They take money! I also knew that hard work is the key to continued success.

I do not mean by hard work manual labor or long hours. I do mean a full effort put forth during one's lifetime, in this case, to achieve financial success. Yes, in your beginning quest for riches you might have to work two jobs, work long hours, and make many sacrifices, but this lifestyle is only necessary during the early years and can be turned around and become more pleasant as you become more sophisticated and more knowledgeable about where to exert your efforts and spend your time making money work for you.

During my early years of working seven days a week and sacrificing holidays and vacations, I often wondered if my effort was worth it. Well, now that I am free to work for myself and set my own achievement standards, I wonder how I could have asked that question in the first place. The extra cash reserve and established income allow freedom of choice and many long-deserved days off.

I have often interviewed successful millionaires who also stress that money and wealth are not all that important. They say to take it easy and enjoy life; yet when I probe into their beginnings, I soon find that they were workaholics and enjoyed pursuing a dream. And, interestingly, these same millionaires still work—not only for the money but for the pleasure.

When we ask those people who have "made it," they talk of the hard times they encountered in the early stages; yet they endured all the uphill battles and triumphed in financial independence. These same people are also very proud of having weathered the storm and accomplishing their dreams. It is almost as if the harder the battle the more glorious the victory.

You must have faith in your goals. YOU are the only one who will work towards fulfilling your dream.

## THE EVERYONE ELSE'S DREAM SYNDROME

One of the most profound mistakes that I have observed in those who have failed is that they pursued someone else's dream. Many times people do not have faith in their own abilities and tend to listen to the wrong people.

The final measure of any success is achieving that which pleases *you* the most—doing whatever it is that enriches *your* life. So if you never reach your financial levels of satisfaction, at least the trip was worth the while.

## THE "I CAN'T" SYNDROME

We may be so bogged down by our present financial commitments or concerns that we do not dare think about tomorrow. Well, if your level of income is not enough now, can you imagine what you will have if you are disabled or if you retire? You must take a stance and commit yourself to whipping out poverty from your life and eliminating doubt and fears about the future! You must unleash that hero within and crush all fears and self-doubt about having what you desire. And as you set out to accomplish your dreams, do not ever lose sight of your goal.

## THE LACK-OF-IMAGINATION SYNDROME

One of the biggest obstacles to overcome is the crippling effect of self-defeat and lack of imagination. Unlike any other nation on earth, the U.S. economy is specifically structured for the individual to try his or her hand at creating wealth; and if failure occurs, a second chance is available through business subsidies, loans, and joint ventures. Many individuals have great ideas but lack of capital; however, if they knew how to let their ideas be known, they might find a backer who could produce the capital to help their dreams come true.

The more dependency you place on society as a whole to maintain your standard of living and self-esteem, the more vulnerable you are to its changes. For example, a fixed-income job could be hazardous to your wealth by not keeping pace with inflation; conversely, if your job offers just a little spare time, possible after-work hours or weekends, you may have the freedom to invest or start a side business.

Wealth for you is not that far off if you are willing to live and breathe its attainment and if you learn to utilize the proper tools:

| | |
|---|---|
| —your present attitude, | —assessment of resources, |
| —time, | —a plan. |

# SHAPE THE DREAM

Success stories abound: the individual who rose from the parking attendant, at a hotel, to the corporate vice president of the entire enterprise; the starving actor or actress who, after a few fortunate "breaks," changed the future of entertainment throughout the world.

What these people might not have known but learned is that every job or position he or she attained within the business needed someone who was qualified, ambitious, and determined to fulfill the expectations of that particular job. It is no surprise that an individual who has mastered virtually every skill required to run a hotel—or sing a song— will be the most qualified person some day to manage those positions that he previously mastered.

We must realize that it is not the attainment of the goal that creates the person but rather the uncertainty of success which drives him to human perfection. For example:

## HARLAND SANDERS, CREATOR OF A FAMOUS AMERICAN FOOD CHAIN:

- —father died when he was five
- —dropped out of school at age 14
- —worked as a farm hand, streetcar conductor, soldier, cook, and bottle washer; studied law for awhile; sold insurance and tires; ran a ferry boat and filling station
- —THEN turned his first social security check for $105.00 into Kentucky Fried Chicken at the age of 65.

## GERALDINE FERRARO, FIRST WOMAN VICE-PRESIDENTIAL CANDIDATE:

- —immigrant parents
- —father died when she was 8
- —went to college on scholarship
- —worked as an elementary school teacher; went to law school at night; married and had three children
- —1974, 14 years after passing the bar, became Assistant D.A.
- —1978, 4 years later, ran for Congress and won
- —1984, 6 years later, nominated first woman vice president.

Whether you are young or old, low or middle income, your opportunities for success lie within your own imagination. The U.S. government purchased the state of Alaska from Russia for just pennies an acre. Alaska was considered a frozen wasteland, a home for Eskimos and polar bears. Alaska has produced billions of dollars in oil, lumber, and other natural resources.

## THE "HOW CAN I BE SO SELFISH" SYNDROME

At times you may stop and question whether your obsession with financial success is healthy. Is it fair to society as a whole? What about those less fortunate than you? Well, let us take a look at just what your personal efforts to secure your financial future will do for others.

First, you must realize that when an individual—you, for instance— sets out to accomplish financial independence, many other people benefit. Let us start at the point where you decide to invest your money or time into a business venture. The day you or the general partner of a business venture applies for a business license, the local bureaucratic structure gladly takes your money for licenses and fees. Then when the business holds inventory or makes a profit, who collects the taxes? Obviously, the city or county tax collectors, the state income tax board, and—of course—the Internal Revenue Service. All these civil service organizations employ thousands of workers whose sole source of income comes from city, county, state, or federal employment. The self-employment (Social Security taxes), income, and propery taxes that the different organizations collect from people like you and me also fund welfare and social aid programs. The income you generate through taxes will be shared by others, and that is just the beginning.

Any major equipment investment in your business, the purchase of operating supplies, the use of manpower, the rental or purchase of space to work in all provide income for employees and professionals who make money off your business.

If you purchase, say, stocks and bonds or real estate, not only will the brokers earn income commissions, but they in turn employ secretaries, accountants, attorneys, advertising agencies, office space and office supply companies.

Many people and organizations thrive because of your efforts. In fact, people like you who take all the risks of generating capital through investing or running businesses support this economy. When you invest your time and money into the American economy, everyone benefits— from the low-income welfare recipients to the high-income wage earners.

So please do not feel any guilt for wanting the finer things in life. If you succeed, you will have put food on the tables of many Americans in the process.

And thus:

# Step 3.2: Adjust Your Attitude to "I Can."

An important accomplishment in your journey is to realize that others, much like you, have made millions of dollars over a lifetime in much the same manner you may set out to do in yours. You need to accept the reality that money is all around you, but it must first be detected and extracted. You need to convince yourself that your dreams are achievable, your goals are obtainable, and your commitment is unbreakable.

Once you have created a forceful and positive attitude, everything else in your life will fall into place. Choices and decisions abound. With a little thought and research (look before you leap), proper decisions and choices can put you in a strong and positive position ready to make the journey of your life down the Road to Prosperity.

After much discussion with self-made wealthy people, I have realized that they tend to be or do the following:

1. They tend to be doers with a great amount of self-motivation.

2. They possess the virtue of reliability.

3. A positive attitude is expressed throughout all their ventures, even when things seem the gloomiest.

4. Willingness to accept new ideas and try new concepts places them apart from those "who will not see."

5. They possess the ability to delegate authority so that they are not actually doing the work but are managing several other individuals' efforts to maximizing their all-out effort.

6. They tend to make sure they have all the facts before venturing into an unknown; however, when they are comfortable that all the necessary research is complete, they will take the plunge with no regrets.

7. They are aware of the risks of producing large sums of money out of just an idea or a small amount of funds. They categorize the risks and accept the outcome and will repeat their actions if necessary—even after experiencing a loss.

8. The final and most important feature that I have observed about the wealthy is that they don't lose track of their assets and a plan for the future. These people really think about what they are doing and plan out a basic strategy—or game plan.

When admiring the accomplishments of others, you must begin to observe how they succeeded, formulate a few ideas of your own, and determine how you will succeed. Just as they succeeded, you can and will achieve *your* dream. You will marshall the stamina to continue when others give up, not yielding your dream no matter what challenging obstacles get in your way.

One of the biggest obstacles that I had while attempting to overcome the boundaries of low income was truly believing in my dream. While working a second job on weekends and being exhausted for the remainder of the week, I actually began to believe that this was going to be my destiny for the rest of my life. But I persisted—in great part out of habit. Then when I first discontinued the weekend work, as I had planned to, I had tremendous trouble accepting the fact that I had the weekend off. I began to feel guilty for not working so hard physically. I didn't know what to do with myself!

Well, I soon began to put the extra time into my business and ended a year of the highest income level in the history of my career. I soon learned that wealth is not achieved necessarily by working hard; it is achieved by thinking for yourself and remaining independent.

Think about it. You are much like a gold prospector in the hills. He must dig up some earth before he can find his fortune. Prosperity will not come to you; you must go to prosperity. You must be your own motivator, friend, and fan club. Those same people who disagreed with my values of hard work and prosperity now envy my independence.

Which brings us to:

## Step 3.3: Review and Revise Your Present Lifestyle

With your financial goals in mind,

1. Review your present financial situation. Define/Identify/ Determine your income, assets, expenses.

2. Reduce or eliminate any unnecessary or excessive spending. I mean this! Dollars saved may be invested in such a way that they act as the first "hidden" resource for saving and investing.

3. Evaluate your present spending habits. Research less expensive ways or places to purchase what you do need.

4. Evaluate your present employment status or business. Determine whether you feel there is a future in potential profits

equal to the hours spent on the job. Determine how secure your present job is. Although a secure job may not pay extremely high wages, it will allow you to make long-term investment commitments, e.g., real estate or small business loans. If your present job lacks a high degree of security and/or potential income, explore what else might be available. Conversely, a private business may have potential for larger profits for investing, but the future may not be as predictable.

Regardless of your present situation—whether it be unpredictable or secure—you should evaluate your individual potential for creating income through your professional commitment.

5. Evaluate the quantity and use of your spare time. The amount of spare time you have in your life is an asset in itself. Any additional time you have each week can be put to improving your chances of making money by working an additional job, improving educational qualifications, or taking up an income-producing hobby. Many people think that a flat 40 hours a week is all an individual needs to spend earning income. Think again!

6. Consider upgrading your skills or extending your potential through additional education. In a high-tech society, you need to become specialized and indispensable. Your knowledge is an investment in your career and future. Just as products and services are changing, expertise and personnel will change. Protect your position by being one step ahead. Do not fall into the misconception that you are still on the job because the company is loyal. As soon as profits fall, companies cut back, and your salary is not immune from the chopping block. Protect your position by being involved and by upgrading your qualifications.

7. Consider expanding your social horizons. The company you keep and friends you see many times have an impact on your realm of imagination. While your family and friends should be valued, consider also rubbing shoulders with those who are successful and could share some of their success stories and ideas with you.

8. Determine your basic financial requirements. The obvious are food and shelter, but what about family protection? income protection? the children's education? the parents' 50th wedding anniversary?

9. Review all the worst things that can happen in your life and determine specifically which of those are already protected against loss. Determine which of these risks you are able and willing to insure against by way of family financial support, back-up savings, or insurance policies. For if, while in the early years of your financial plan, you are medically disabled, lose a close family member, have a year in which your income is low or insufficient, or just come across a new and exciting opportunity, you should have a plan and resources that will rise to the occasion, thus preventing you from having to deplete your present assets. If you have a good-sized nest egg and cover all the bases, success in whatever you do is more easily attainable.

10. Assess your goals and strive for those which are realistically attainable given your present and future resources.

Having recognized some of the hard work and sacrifices ahead and having taken a hard look at your style of living and the money you have available, you are now ready to:

## Step 3.4: Touch Base With Your Personal-Comfort Tolerance Level for Day-to-Day Living

There is little joy in being miserable. Obviously, to achieve wealth, you will have to make some sacrifices—leisure time, vacations, new living room draperies, Saturday nights out. How much you are willing to sacrifice depends on your—and your family's—ability to tolerate "deprivation."

One man's deprivation is, of course, another's sense of well-being. Just bear in mind, as you identify what *you* can tolerate, that "every penny saved is a penny earned."

And so the dream takes shape. You know what you have already and you have identified what standard of living will be comfortable for you as you travel the road to economic freedom. You are now ready to begin.

# STEP 4:
# EXECUTE THE DREAM

Some time ago in this adventure you said to yourself: I am an aspiring millionaire. I am not there yet, but based on my resources and especially my intent, arrival is inevitable. I will reach my destination. The only question is, how soon?

Soon is the answer. You have already begun. By looking inward, you have learned who you are and where you want to go and how you want to be. You have explored the obstacles in your way and begun to disassemble them. You are developing a new and positive attitude. Are you ready?

Yes.

You are ready to take your dream, your awareness of obstacles, your new attitude and begin concrete action:

## Step 4.1: Create the Budget That Accommodates Both the Reality and the Dream

Most every millionaire monitors his expenses. That strategy put him where he is now.

To get *you* started, you will find budget worksheets in Appendix A.

Creating and following a budget has two important advantages. First, it forces you to learn to spend only as much money as you have allocated for various expenditures each month. Second, it reduces the amount of money wasted through needless expenditures. For example, instead of wasting the extra $50 you are left with each month after expenses, you can allocate it to an IRA for tax-free interest or save it up to purchase a new car.

---

### EXAMPLE OF THE PRODUCTIVITY OF THE $50 YOU SAVED IN A MONTH
($50 a month earning 10% interest)

| | | |
|---|---|---|
| In  5 years | = | $ 3,904 |
| In 10 years | = | $10,327 |
| In 20 years | = | $38,284 |

---

This type of long-term budgeted savings could provide something as important as your child's education.

By allowing you to look at all of your spending alternatives, budgeting requires that you set some goals. An effective budget is one that provides a means for you to improve or maintain your lifestyle the way that you and your family wish. It can help you buy the things you want by planning for expenditures and controlling them.

Budgeting does not necessarily mean that you must follow a strict financial diet; it just means that you record your expenditures. By visualizing—recording—these expenditures, you can realize where you have "gone astray" or overextended yourself.

When reviewing—recording—your spending habits, another important practice is that of collecting receipts and maintaining tax records. You should be fully familiar with what items are tax-deductible. Each dollar of necessary expenses that qualifies could save you around thirty cents, depending on your tax bracket. For some people, especially the small business owners, those receipts can save thousands of dollars come tax time.

Your most effective weapon against poverty is the control of expenditures. The most valuable tool for the creation of wealth is the ability to invest. Both talents will lead you down the path of prosperity and happiness.

## Step 4.2: Find out Everything You Can About What's out There in the World of Money

It is often said, "Knowledge is king." If you take two people with no money to their names and place them in a crowded city, the one without knowledge will go hungry while the one with knowledge and self-confidence will seek out all recources, put them to work, and soon be among the wealthy and envied because he or she had all the so-called "breaks." Knowledge can break you free from the chains of financial dependence and allow you to create a self-made world of confidence and self-esteem.

Where do you acquire the knowledge you need?

1. Parts II and III of this book provide you with a base for understanding money, various investments, and planning. Read it as a start. Refer back to it whenever necessary.

2. Any number of investment seminars are available in most metropolitan areas through banks, credit unions, investment companies, adult ed programs. However, unless you pay to attend these classes or seminars, you will most likely be asked

invest in something; and before you invest, you need to complete this book and have a clear plan for your financial future.

3. Biographies and financial journals provide an exploration of various ways individuals—like you—have become successful. As you are doing your "research," you will undoubtedly come in contact with three basic methods that have proven successful.

   1) Real estate, a very lucrative field in the long run but dangerous for the inexperienced. Beware of "get rich quick" schemes.

   2) Your own business, an adventure that can bring great pleasure and future profits but must be well thought out and continually attended in order to guarantee productivity.

   3) New product invention.

   In all success stories you will find that the successful looked around carefully, determined what people needed or wanted, and then filled that need.

4. Read the financial pages of the newspaper.

## Step 4.3: Create a Financial Plan

You are about to enter the most important phase of your trip to millionaire status. Whether your resources provide an earlier arrival than most or taking risks is in the cards, the specific byways and rest stops will all become apparent in the financial plan. Most financial problems occur because people don't think through their actions and consider the ultimate outcome. Planning helps us make tough, effective decisions and be more successful.

## Step 4.4: Review and Revise Your Financial Plan As You Go

Times change. Not only will the market fluctuate, but also your needs will vary as circumstances—and the market—alter. Therefore, it is imperative that you constantly review what you are doing and revise accordingly.

The plan itself?

Read on.

**PART II**
# THE FINANCIAL PLANNER AND THE PLAN

26

Hearst Castle, CA

Hearst Castle, CA

# I
# A FEW BASICS ABOUT PLANNING

Before moving a muscle toward your financial future, you will need some grounding in what to expect and how to think.

A few of the basics are:

## The Plan in Pictures

Ideally, a financial plan (or investment portfolio or estate plan—there are many names) resembles a pyramid.

Speculative
programs.

Growth stocks, oil and gas,
realty funds, real estate,
personally owned businesses, etc.

Money market funds, government securities,
retirement programs, and blue chip stocks.

At the pyramid's very broad base are conservative investments, which provide liquidity and safety of principal, and a few conservative investments that have growth potential. In its center are average-risk investments. And at the top, speculation begins.

The proportional density of the layers of the pyramid is determined by you—your age, needs, goals, and comfort level. For some of you, greater risk is a challenge, and so the top is larger. For others, safety is uppermost, and the base predominates. For one and all, because of its broad base, the pyramid is not likely to topple over.

## Traveling Two Roads at Once

Yes, you can travel two roads at once.

One is a conservative, long-distance road that requires a diligent savings and investment program which takes into consideration the risks of inflation. Long-term planning assures the nest egg will be protected from all sorts of economic changes. This asset plan grows by regular additions and deposits. Some risks are taken, but safety is a major consideration.

On the other hand, if you are on track for your long-term goals and you have excess time, money, and contingency programs for emergencies, you can pursue a more aggressive attitude and seek faster ways of reaching your goal.

Phase 1 will look like this:

## Phase 1/ Conservative

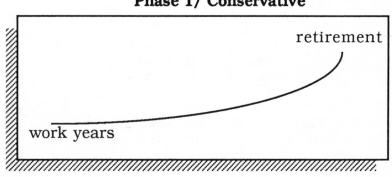

retirement

work years

You will notice a slow but gradual line that inclines on a consistent basis—a conservative direction that will insure your long-term goal of reaching millionaire status. This plan is achieved by a long-term, slow-but-sure estate growth of asset accumulation.

Phase 1 takes advantage of basic money management concepts. This plan specializes in savings and investment plans that are more likely to retain their value in the future and historically have increased in value over time. Examples of Phase 1 plans are real estate for all cash with no loans existing; retirement programs such as an IRA; bonds, utility stocks; and blue chip stocks. The goal is to build a base of savings-like investments that can be liquidated if needed. Phase 1 is more concerned with the eventual achievement of your goal than the time period of completion.

A basic mode for establishing Phase 1 direction is:

Save

Invest in retirement programs

Purchase residence

Purchase investments

Establish side business

SAVE — Acquiring a substantial savings base gives you the comfort of security and allows you freedom from the normal restraints of money. The savings base is not limited to a bank account and may include some money-market or tax-free-bond accounts. It is money available for any opportunity or emergency that might occur and frees you from the whim of fate in time of need.

RETIREMENT PROGRAMS — By participating in whatever retirement plans are available to you, you will know that no matter what goes wrong outside the retirement plans, you will be able to retire when you desire and, if all goes according to plan, at millionaire status. In the meantime, you have established a "last resort emergency fund" while reducing your tax liability.

RESIDENCE — Purchasing your own residence is not considered an investment, but simply a way to lock in your expenses by paying a set mortgage payment that some day allows you the total peace of mind of no rent or house payments at all. It also helps to reduce income taxes because of property tax and mortgage interest deductions.

INVESTMENTS — Next, purchasing investments allows you the ability to put your money to work on a seven-day-a-week, 24-hour-a-day basis. Since your retirement programs should be conservative in nature, your investment program can afford to be more aggressive, structured for growth, and protect you from inflation.

SIDE BUSINESS — Establishing a side business is an important achievement which can bring you that much closer to Phase 2. You can now afford to be much more aggressive assuming you already have a job, have reduced your expenses, and have been saving and investing for the future. At this point, a small business failure won't really damage your future goals. However, if you become involved in something that could grow and become successful, and if you continue using thoughtful basic money management techniques you mastered along the way, you are now ready for Phase 2.

In starting a small business, first look for something that will not immediately conflict with your present job and does not require a lot of capital. Be careful, there are a lot of scams that claim you can buy a franchise and strike it rich. The facts are you must pay someone a large franchise fee and purchase his supplies for inventory. There are, however, alternatives to the scam. For example, many people in the mid-1970's made good money as part-time real estate agents.

Some advice on starting a small business: Stay away from anything that you are not knowledgeable in and do not fancy yourself in, for if you are going to labor over a business for a few years, you had better like the work you are going to be doing. Bear in mind, failure can occur if you start out inexperienced, under-funded, and short on patience and cash flow necessary to weather several years of "apprenticeship."

That brings us to the end of Phase 1. Phase 2 will look like this:

### Phase 2/ Aggressive

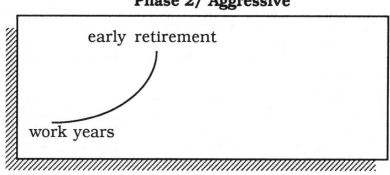

In this phase of the plan, life becomes a little more exciting. After doing your chores (so to speak) and doing all the right things in Phase 1 in order to insure a successful long-term plan, you can now start dealing with the possibility of success on a short-term basis. You can now go where you have never ventured before, try ideas that others won't dare, risk the fate of failure, and laugh in the face of fear. You now have all your bases covered, and nothing can bring you down.

So where do you go from here, you ask? Well, where would you like to go?

Some people might simply choose to become more aggressive in their investments. For example, they might try buying real estate for low or no money down and attempt to speculate in the market. They might even begin to purchase aggressive growth stocks in the market using various buying and selling techniques. Others might like to take the success of the part-time business of Phase 1 and expand it into a full-sized business or profession. Whichever direction you decide to take, bear in mind the following:

1. There are always opportunities—in bad times as well as good times. If you own an investment that is presently down in value or price but is sound, what better time to buy more? Buy more while everyone else is negative on the idea. When the investment becomes more popular and the price rises, sell to those who lacked your foresight. Regardless of the investment, there are buyers and there are sellers.

2. Creating an aggressive investment portfolio and expanding a business are similar activities. Both must be watched very closely and nurtured along the way. Both might require the investment of additional monies in order to outlive the down cycles.

3. If you are inclined to continue in business for yourself, make sure you are in an industry that will always be needed. There are exceptions to this rule, of course. If you are the type of person who likes the challenge and risks of timing your product or service with the demands of the public, you can get a quick boost to prosperity with a short-lived fad—if you get lucky.

4. If you choose a business that requires a slow but gradual growth of clientele, treat your customers in such a way that they will learn to respect your professionalism and integrity. Be good, honest, reliable, sincere, and believe in what you are doing. The better you treat your present customers, the better chance you have of keeping them and also receiving new business through referrals.

5. Look around you. People have made millions of dollars overnight by creating businesses that have withstood the test of time. I met a millionaire who, a few years ago, was just as ordinary as you or I. He was working seven days a week and trying to think of a business or idea that could boost his long-term effort into instant profits. This same person now has several large assets and businesses. Instead of a fancy car, he owns a jet aircraft. Can you believe that?

I remember meeting another person dressed in garage overalls with a name patch on his pocket. Come to find out, this person owned the largest and most prestigious custom auto body and paint shop in town, was nationally known, and worth millions. What did he do to earn his fortunes? He did what he knew and loved, he refurbished cars to their originality. What allowed him to become a millionaire while others in the same business could only dream of such success? It was the obsession for perfection in the quality of his work and the satisfaction of his customers. This person is now retired; and—guess what!—with all his free time, he restores old cars in his custom shop at the rear of his estate. Remember what I mentioned earlier? You have got to enjoy what you do.

Another individual I know liked sales. Years ago he began selling real estate. Living from sale to sale, he soon learned that personal money management was important because he never knew when he would have feast or famine. As time when on, the opportunity arose to purchase the real estate company he worked for with a couple of his friends. In time he and his partners purchased several properties, just as any good salesperson should, to show customers that they believed in their product. However, even though the original plan of purchasing good investment properties at low prices would have produced profits in the long term, lo and behold the real estate boom of the mid- and late 1970s arrived. This boom caused the single greatest increase in value in the history of California real estate. And a conservative accumulation plan turned into a gold mine.

6. In most success stories you will find that the individual became involved with the investment or business because of a prior knowledge or liking for that venture. Since it takes years to complete the investment cycle, you must surely enjoy what you are doing and be willing to deflect everyone else's doubts and negative attitudes.

Phase 1 and Phase 2 together look like this:

## Phase 3/ Combined

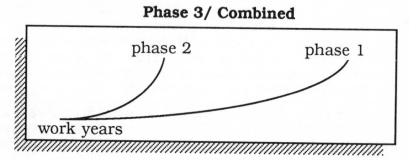

How does it look to you? You can satisfy the conservative concerns you may have as you feed that desire to attain entrepreneur status with an idea of your own. Whether you become a successful investor or business person, you will always remember where you came from. This new status did not just happen; you made it happen and not without a lot of work and sacrifice.

## The Four Estates

The basics of any financial plan will include the following areas that we call "The Four Estates." I have provided an in-depth analysis of specific areas that affect them so that the needs and parameters of your movements toward your lifetime goals and present responsibilities can be determined.

### PRESENT ESTATE

This estate concerns your present standard of living. In other words, where you are right now financially: your expenses, assets, liabilities, and estimated taxes for the current year. The goal for this estate is to maintain or increase your standard of living; to keep up with potential changes in inflation, deflation, recession, or any other economic changes which may occur; and to reduce your taxes.

This estate is made up of some very basic concepts and documents: budget, balance sheet/net worth statement, and tax estimate.

*Budgeting*, as discussed in Step 4, enables you to project future expenses and resources in order to identify any diversification possibilities, determine net growth, and project income tax strategy. A monthly budget is an extremely important tool to use in a financial plan. It is a detailed description of family expenses and allocations of income to cover these expenses. You know how much money you bring home each month from your paycheck, but a budget is important because it helps you keep track of what goes out. If you don't know what goes out on a monthly basis, it is difficult to determine whether there will be any extra dollars each month for you to put into savings and investment plans.

Some people realize that they need a budget when they don't have the money to buy something that they need or want. For others, the consequences are more serious. Their lack of financial management causes them to run out of money before the next paycheck, and, consequently, they cannot pay their bills.

*The balance sheet or net worth statement.* One of the most

important steps in determining your present financial status is the completion of the balance sheet. While businesses consider a balance sheet essential to financial survival, it is a foreign object to most people. A balance sheet is a list of what you own and what you owe. It gives you an idea of where you stand financially.

After you subtract the liabilities (bills) from the assets (investments), you will discover your net balance (net worth) and can monitor how much debt you have incurred and whether or not to change plans about future expenditures.

In recording assets, you may discover assets forgotten about, such as personal property, jewelry, or the value of a small business. If you record not only what you have but also account numbers, locations of assets, and instructions, you can eliminate severe inconveniences, emotional pain, and perhaps expense for your family in case of an emergency.

The balance sheet is similar to a doctor's full physical examination except the balance sheet reveals your financial health. Just as a doctor needs to know everything about you to determine and insure your health, you must know everything about your finances in order to obtain financial stability.

A worksheet is provided for your use in Appendix A.

*Taxes.* One of the biggest concerns of Americans today is the increasing size of their tax liabilities. A financial plan can help you reduce your tax bill.

The first step in reducing taxes is to evaluate your current situation. You will need to know everything about your present income—including wages, investment gains, dividends, and interest; and your deductions— home interest expense, rental property, and other personal write-offs. Having the proper information and figures will enable you or a consulting accountant/financial planner to identify your present tax bracket and estimate future taxes.

Regardless of the current tax laws, there will always be tax incentives that can help you reduce your future tax liabilities. By evaluating your present tax liabilities, you discover areas for savings. For example, if you lack a stable retirement plan where you work and still need a tax shelter, obviously the perfect tax shelter to provide maximum tax write-off with minimum risk would be something like an IRA. However, once you venture beyond conservative retirement funds, additional tax shelter from other investments requires certain commitments. After running additional tax estimates to determine the after-tax effect of investing in certain tax shelters or properties, you can decide whether the after-tax result will be worthwhile. If purchasing another real estate property reduces your tax slightly but the extra work in maintaining the property is going to be substantial, the tax estimate might help you make your decision. This testing procedure can only be done when you know what your present situation is and what future changes to plan for. Remember, every method of recording tax deductions could put money in your pocket and out of those whose owners would gladly spend it for you, like the IRS.

## DEATH ESTATE

Death is inevitable. Everyone knows or will experience the family stress associated with death and definitely will not need the additional burden of worrying about finances. For this reason, it is important to properly plan for your loved ones.

The death estate needs to provide income to survivors from either current assets or the proceeds of life insurance. Basically, you need to determine how much you have in your current assets and how much your family will need to live on if you pass away.

All conceivable sources of income should be considered. If other family members would be willing to help out, who and how? If you have life insurance, what kind and how much? (The mistake of incorrect amounts and value: cost ratio of life insurance is an on-going problem and will be taken up in Part III, V.)

One consolation about this section of planning is the peace of mind that comes from knowing you have protected your family: It will remain intact and preserve your dream if something should happen to you. This comfort makes the unpleasantness worthwhile.

## DISABILITY ESTATE

Fact: *Disability is the single largest destroyer of income and assets today.*

Fact: *A disabled person continues to be a consumer in need of special attention and consideration while not producing any income.*

In order to protect yourself against financial disaster in the event you become disabled, you will need a disability income protection program provided through employment or private plan, or sufficient assets to generate maintenance income. Unfortunately, when families plan their financial futures, the disability estate is often forgotten. If you overlook this estate, the end result can be emotionally and financially devastating.

There are several ways to provide a reliable source of income for yourself in the event you become disabled.

1. *Social Security*. Many people believe they can rely on social security if they become disabled, but since strict requirements apply, only the severely disabled are able to collect:

1) The disability must be total and be expected to last at least 12 months.

2) The disability or impairment must be so severe that the worker is unable to engage in any substantially gainful work.

In addition, the benefits are not ample.

Assume a 34-year-old wage earner with a spouse and three children currently makes $35,000 a year. If he suffers a disability, he will receive income from social security as follows:

Approximately $950 per month until the children reach 18; then benefits are reduced to

approximately $635 per month until he reaches age 65 and begins receiving his regular retirement benefits.

Also, don't always count on Social Security for disability income. Many reports say that thousands are turned down for benefits each year. Although many states have short-term coverage, it expires within a year.

2. *Use your savings*. This scheme can only temporarily ease your financial problem and can destroy the plans you had for the future, which was what the money was intended for.

3. *Borrow the money*. How much? For how long? And who would be willing to lend money to you—a disabled person who may never be able to generate income?

4. *Liquidate your assets*. Imagine being forced to sell your car, jewelry, even your home in order to bring in money to support you and your family. This would obviously destroy your plans for the future.

5. *Income security plan*. This provides tax-free replacement income during a period of disability caused by accident or sickness. Considering

the benefits provided, a disability plan is surprisingly low in cost. The amount of income, length of coverage period, and starting date after you become disabled can usually be tailored to your needs. Unfortunately, disability protection must be supplemented by other sources if the family doesn't want to make drastic changes in its standard of living. Check to see what plan your employer provides; chances are it won't be enough.

Planning for a disability is probably the most abused area of planning. Just as people do not want to think about death, neither do they like to think about disability. However, many disabled Americans suffer a more crippling disease than the disability itself: guilt—the feeling that they are a major burden to their family and others. Planning for the worst eventuality frees the individual to think creatively, without guilt, about achieving millionaire status.

## RETIREMENT ESTATE

Data released by the Social Security Administration reveals a sad statistic that has remained fairly constant over the past nine years: 95% of all those aged 65 or over currently maintain a standard of living with a total income of $9,000 per year or less. That statistic translates to — only 5% of the people aged 65 or over are self-supporting. The remainder depend on help from relatives and charity or are compelled to work in order to sustain themselves. I have met people who were at retirement age, yet couldn't retire. They were forced to live a life of continuous financial uncertainty.

Frightening? Yes. This fourth estate needs serious attention.

Planning for your retirement will determine whether or not your "golden years" will really be golden. Ideally, the goal is to maintain your current standard of living when retired.

But how?

Recognize that Social Security was never meant to be the sole means of support for the retired. The average benefit is usually at or below the poverty line and if you earn over a certain amount, your social security benefits will be cut in proportion to your income. Therefore, you will need to receive income from your investments.

A financial plan can help ensure that you have enough money for your retirement. Your pre-retirement investment portfolio will be different from your retirement investment portfolio, but your assets should not shrink. At retirement, losing assets to various risks can destroy independence, for unlike the young person who can go back to work and recreate an investment portfolio, the retired individual does not have another chance. The retiree needs to create an "overkill" portfolio, more money than what is actually needed.

If at retirement, you reposition assets to a conservative, low risk of loss, you need another type of insurance—inflation protection. Inflation can be protected by one of two things: 1) assets invested in areas that rise with inflation, such as stocks, real estate, gold (unfortunately, these same inflation-hedged investments run the risk of loss in a recession); and 2) an overkill of assets. If you want to own government securities that are not at risk to dollar loss, you will need far more money invested to fight inflation because your invested dollars will not increase in value and will only earn a consistent interest income. The cost of living in the real world might rise far above what the nest-egg plan provides.

Consider the amount you will receive from pensions, if any. Your pension, social security, IRA, and investment income should total the amount you need plus an inflation factor. If your projected income equals or exceeds your desired income, then you have nothing to worry about. However, if your total income falls short of your goals—which is usually the case—you will have to sit down and decide how to make up for the short fall. To make additional savings and investment strategies, sacrifices and alternative income sources may be needed.

## THE FOUR ESTATES SUMMARIZED

As you can see, before you can begin plans for the future, you must first understand your present financial position. By knowing how your monthly expenses affect your ability to save and invest for the future, present bills can be retired and future responsibilities taken on; taxes can be modified and assets used to restructure your future. After gaining a perspective of your present financial position, you need to consider the serious contingencies pointed out in the death, disability, and retirement estates. People do die every day; others become disabled; and many more are not able to retire at all in their so-called golden years.

Look around you. Ask questions of your friends and their elderly relatives. The lack of funds during emergencies and at retirement has humiliated many a proud American. Money isn't everything, but it surely eases the pressures brought on by the lack of it.

# II

# THE FINANCIAL PLANNER

As you drive the road to financial success, you most definitely need a financial plan.

The question is, do you need a financial planner?

Maybe not—if you are willing to structure the plan today; if you are well versed in finances and the market; if you have great amounts of time to monitor, study up, focus on what's out there; if you can remain objective, stand back, and clinically analyze what you are doing.

Probably yes—if you tend to procrastinate; if you are just beginning; if your knowledge of financial considerations is limited; if you are confused about money's potential; if you question your capacity to remain analytical and objective.

A financial planner is a professional who is trained in money management, who continually studies the availability of new products and the shifts in focus of the old. He monitors and manages an updating of your financial plan, and serves as a sounding board for and researcher of investment possibilities. He makes a firm commitment to your success.

Perhaps the most important of the financial planner's skills is his trained objectivity. This factor of objectivity is important because when our emotions are engaged, our thinking and reasoning tend to cloud up, and our feelings tend to kick in when we engage in money matters. Will we succeed or won't we? Will we lose face? Will Uncle Henry laugh and tell us he told us so? Our feelings can make us financially overly cautious, flamboyant, careless, or impotent. As a rule, surgeons do not operate on family members. Attorneys do not defend their sons, daughters, wives.

Equal in significance is that the financial planner does today what we might do tomorrow. Financial planning—or the creating of a plan on a yearly basis—is not required by the local or federal government as is a tax return. A tax return is compulsory. The government is extremely interested in what we make each year because the bureaucrats in Washington like to spend the money we pay in taxes. They are seldom concerned about how much money we hang on to or whether we will have enough income at retirement. Because there is neither the threat of a fine nor the fear of imprisonment for the failure to prepare and follow a financial plan each year, most people tend to put it off.

# The Criteria for Selecting a Financial Planner

If you decide to work with a planner, there are several qualifications to consider. Because the field is literally in its infancy, you need to be very cautious in making a decision about whom to trust. Preferably, when choosing a planner, find someone else who has worked with one and recommends him. I don't want to scare you away from this profession, but I do want to point out a few basics so you can make an informed decision.

## METHOD OF PAYMENT

First, consider the method of his or her "salary." There are basically three types of compensation.

1. The planner is fee based. She/he is paid strictly on fees, much like an attorney or accountant. When the work is done, you are billed.

2. The investment broker gives free advice and financial planning. He is only paid if you invest in his products or investment programs.

3. The planner does both. He constructs a financial plan for a fee that might be a little more reasonable than that of the fee-only person because he is hoping that you will like the plan and the services rendered and will invest with him.

If the planner is fee based, you should realize that his or her time is very valuable and you should be willing to pay for consultations, analysis, and phone calls that are provided for you. Some clients find this too picky; they would like to talk with their planner without cost and depend on this person on a more casual basis. If a planner is going to be available on a casual basis, he is going to have to make up for the time spent with you by making a commission at some other time. This is not so bad; any sales-oriented profession tends to treat its clientele very well because of the hidden treasures that might exist in happy clients and their referrals.

## EDUCATION

The training and educational background of planners vary quite a bit because of the newness of the profession. However, there are a few areas that provide adequate training or qualifications.

1. *Masters in Business Administration (MBA).* This is a very impressive college degree that provides several classes in

economics, investments, personal money management, and financial planning.

2. *Certified Financial Planner (CFP)*. This is a correspondence course that takes about two years for completion. It is much harder than it sounds. The applicant takes quarterly exams that test his knowledge and creativity in creating a personal financial plan.

3. *Registered Investment Advisor*. This is a national-type registration of individuals who make a living giving investment advice to individuals and institutions. Here the Securities Exchange Commission, unannounced, can audit an individual to determine if that person is in compliance with the rules and regulations set forth by law. This person is required to have certain licenses and have a minimum amount of experience in the field, not to mention the securities' licensing exams required.

When working with anyone who would profit by your investing with him, you need to evaluate your relationship and trust before accepting advice on what to do with your money. As in any profession, people who are not as professional as would be preferred, practice financial planning. This is because the profession is very new and the non-differentiation between those who actually practice financial planning and those who use the term as a buzz word to sell securities and insurance still exists.

Many financial planners and professional organizations are structured to maintain the integrity for all, but as with any profession where the client must trust the professional, we must all be careful.

## TRUST

The most important element is that you feel comfortable with the planner. Does this person appear to be honest and place your needs above his or hers? You don't want someone who is eager to make a commission from your investing to advise you regarding the size of your cash reserve. Why? This person might know that you should keep your money in cash for an emergency, but if he is greedy, he will advise you to invest the cash with him. Now, who is he thinking of first?

Please don't think that all financial planners are like the previous example. They are not. It's those few "bad apples" that make choosing difficult.

Bear in mind that the planner may not always have good news after evaluating your financial situation. He or she might suggest that you cut up your credit cards, stop spending so much money, or even get a second job. If you are going to get on the right track for capital accumulation, you must find a person whom you will not only trust but also listen to and follow the advice of.

Once you find a good financial planner, you should take it upon yourself to give this individual all the support you can muster. The development of good professionals who will look out for your well being instead of their own is a public concern. The greedy persons who call themselves planners can be eliminated by your supporting those planners whom you like and trust. And, of course, if you like and trust this person, you will be working with him for some time into the future and you will want him to be very successful on his own so you do not lose him to some large corporation. If your relationship with the planner goes well, chances are you will be working with that individual for the rest of your life.

## The Process

The planner will review your present, death, disability, and retirement estates by reviewing your insurance coverages, your current investments and savings, your current assets, and your goals and objectives in each estate.

Roughly, he proceeds as follows:

1. Based on full disclosure and documentation that you provide, he reviews all financial facts. After playing the role of financial investigator and investment counselor, the planner has a clear picture of your overall situation.

2. He maps out various alternatives and plans an overview of the various directions you might follow.

3. He sits down with you and reviews all of the areas of concern and points out problem areas that need to be discussed. This session is objective and unbiased. He simply suggests a few alternatives you might consider.

4. He consolidates all of your alternatives and maps out a direction to follow.

5. Throughout the planning process, he reviews the goals and objectives and possibilities with you in order to assure you that your feelings and desires are being served.

6. He monitors your financial progress as you proceed and continues to inform you of market possibilities.

Whether you choose to create your financial plan on your own or work with a financial planner, remember that it is *your* plan, that *you* need to know the possibilities and the dream so that *you* can make informed decisions about how to make *your* money grow and serve you well.

# III

# THE FINANCIAL PLAN

Because the two go hand in hand, I will address the financial plan in the context of the planner. This will also give you a better sense of how to evaluate the effectiveness and integrity of a planner.

The goal of the counseling process is to define, describe, and evaluate the status of the four estates (present, death, disability, and retirement) to obtain the maximum profitability from each. By reviewing all estates, the planner gets an idea of which area to concentrate his efforts in to create the best financial plan for you, a plan that will achieve the best results.

As with any process, there is a beginning to the planning process. Remember all that thinking and dreaming and learning you did earlier? Well, you will need it now. You will need your dreams in all their specifics, your new attitude, your adjusted lifestyle, your budget and asset sheets, your new-found knowledge of the money world—and all your financial and legal documents!—in order to begin the data session.

## Data Session

Before a plan can be constructed, an inspection and analysis of your present financial status must be done. Some questions to address include:

—What will happen to your financial status if the bread winner dies, becomes disabled, or lives long enough to need an extended retirement fund?

—Where will funds come from to support your family in an emergency?

—What is your present net worth and liabilities?

—What will your tax liability be?

—What are your present budget requirements and investment resources?

This inspection will give the planner an idea of your current financial situation and provide a base to begin construction of your financial plan.

By documenting and calculating your current resources and including your current and possible future needs, you will be able to establish a direction that will better fit your particular situation. It's almost impossible for me to advise people what to do with their financial lives until I have had a chance to determine where they now stand financially and where they want to go. This area of planning may not be exhilarating and exciting at first; yet if left undone, it can be the one weak link of the chain and bring you tumbling down to a poverty level and the worst disappointments and frustrations you can imagine.

After the data session with you, the planner begins planning using various types of services: market research, security analysis, and opinions of both financial and legal experts. (When dealing with a professional financial planner, there may be a fee for these services which will be discussed in your initial consultation. Also discussed in the opening session will be disclosures explaining whether or not the planner is licensed to broker investments and insurance products on his own.)

A vehicle for accomplishing the planning work is the

## Investment Analysis

Many people invest their money in various programs without knowing all the facts. The less knowledge you have of an investment, the more risk you are taking. Most financial advisors will suggest that you first determine whether or not you should invest at all. Then they will consider what type of investment you need and how your overall finances will be affected. It is then, and only then, that the proper investment companies should be sought out with the help of reliable and trustworthy investment brokers.

The area of the financial plan that is perhaps the most interesting is this search for better places to put money. There are some basic questions which should be answered during an investment analysis of a specific asset:

1. What exactly is this type of investment?
2. What risks are involved?
3. Are there any tax benefits?
4. Will this trigger an IRS audit?
5. How long am I to be committed?
6. Does it pay me income?
7. Can this investment be liquidated?

These questions are just the tip of the iceberg in an investment analysis.

Within the analysis, it is important to know how much economic diversification there is in your investments. Investing in different areas of the economy can give you liquidity, growth potential, and safety.

Questions must be asked. Is your cash reserve adequate or too large and generating excessive taxes on the income it produces? What is the future purchasing power of the dollars you now have available? Will they keep up with inflation and increase with the cost of living?

You will need to explore the specific details of risk, tax status, and liquidity. Each investment has its own features and characteristics. By knowing the characteristics of your investments, you can better determine if they meet your current and future needs. Whereas safety and liquidity may have been a need in the past, future investment needs may be for growth and tax benefits. These needs can change from year to year.

To determine your needs, you need to review your four estates: present, disability, death, retirement. Every estate affects another. If any of the four estates is deficient, then the investments are affected. For example, if you are unable to purchase disability insurance while working, the investment program should consider the future possibility of a need for liquidity of income if you become disabled. The weak protection you have in one place of a plan must be made up somewhere else. It's an old saying; The "plan" is only as strong as the weakest link in the chain.

When you go in to see a financial planner for a session, you will need to provide as much information and documentation as you can on any investments that you currently hold, may be purchasing in the near future, or may be inheriting one day. You need to know where your investments are located and when they were made and for what reason. You will need to have all insurance policies in hand. This review is necessary because, as stated, investment objectives change from year to year. An investment this year might not fit your needs three years from now.

And always, whether planning with a planner or on your own, you should be interested in your investments, for if you are not concerned, no one else will be. Making millions will be impossible if you are not interested enough to supervise the management of your accumulating estate.

## Asset Repositioning

Having different needs, priorities, and goals is what makes every individual unique. It is the financial planner's responsibility to create and tailor a financial plan to meet these needs. As the needs change, the planner must shift investment strategies to meet the updated financial objectives. This particular task is known as asset repositioning.

Before attempting financial improvement, you must consider current and future taxes, growth, safety, income, liquidity, and retirement. When a planner begins to reposition assets, the client's goals have already been determined, and a full investment analysis of the client's current portfolio has been completed.

Examples of repositioning assets are:

—If tax liability is a problem for a retired person, he might shift his assets from taxable savings accounts to tax-free bonds.

—A person at the peak of his earning capacity might want to take the equity out of his home to expand and broaden his investment base. By using those borrowed funds to buy more investments, an investor expands much as a corporation expands in hopes of creating more profit.

—Safety of assets is especially important for people who must live off the income from their investments. No one likes to lose money, particularly retired people whose most important goal is the preservation of capital. Government-backed securities are appropriate for these people. Investing in real estate may be an additional alternative for inflation protection.

The concept of risk should be closely evaluated. Risk does not simply mean the act of losing (such as an investment in a business that fails). There are other risks that exist and create loss silently, one being inflation. If the cost of living rises and the number of dollars you own does not, you have lost purchasing power. In some cases the loss of purchasing power can be as much as 10% a year. The costs of items and necessities that you plan to purchase in the future can skyrocket. Heating costs, travel, food, and phone bills have been known to rise in cost even in so-called low-inflationary cycles.

Income is top priority for retired persons or anyone else who depends on investment income for subsistence. A great investment would be bonds or bond funds because they provide steady income. The particular type of bond chosen for an investment will depend on the person's secondary goals, such as safety or liquidity. Again, government-backed bonds are the safest, but corporate bonds and bond funds are available for those who are willing to risk a little more for higher income.

Oil income funds and real estate investment trusts also offer a fairly steady income.

Liquidity is a primary concern for people who may need to get to their money fast. Everyone should have some sort of emergency or "rainy day" fund, the size of which depends on the person's needs. The conservative way to maintain this type of fund is to "stick it in a mattress." As a result, this money earns no interest, and with existing inflation, it loses its purchasing power. Passbook savings accounts at banks and savings and loans are not earning much either. The best type of fund which will allow you easy access is a money market mutual fund. There are different types; each provides different advantages compatible with different investment objectives.

With existing inflation, growth is a primary concern for many investors. Almost every type of investment including stocks, mutual funds, oil income funds, and real estate investments can provide growth.

After becoming more familiar with the types of investments available, you must determine what to add depending on your future needs. A soon-to-be-retiring person may reposition his investments from long-term growth vehicles to more conservative income-producing ones. The aspiring millionaire who has played it safe by having a lot of cash around may have a tax problem and need to reposition the cash reserve to more tax-favored investment vehicles.

## Tax Revision Estimates

All of the investments that you make, whether they be treasury bills earning fully taxable income or municipal bonds producing tax-free interest, have some impact on your tax status. If one of your goals is to reduce your taxes, then you must revise your tax estimate as you progress. The planner will suggest various hypothetical situations, and each time a major idea is considered, an income tax revision should be performed. The revision allows you to see exactly how much can be saved in taxes with the specific investment. The investment may or may not be advantageous.

A tax estimate revision progresses as follows:

1. A basic look at your tax liabilities.

2. A revision of your tax estimate by adding some small, tax-saving idea, such as an IRA.

3. A revision of the estimate, if you qualify for an IRA, plus any

other tax-sheltered retirement plan of your own or your employer's.

4. A tax revision taking into account all the above tax deductions plus more sophisticated procedures, such as tax-sheltered investments, home equity loans, charitable gifts, and other tax-saving ideas that fit your situation.

Each time an investment is made, your entire tax situation for that year and those following will be irreversibly changed, hopefully for the better. Thus, careful planning is a must in order to insure benefits and prevent obstacles.

Once various ideas have been explored, you should again review your present situation, goals, and objectives in order to determine when the ideas should be implemented. As mentioned elsewhere in this book, tax deductions are great for reducing taxes, but they are not without strings attached. Certain tax deductions require that you tie up funds (retirement funds), accept low yields (tax-exempt bonds), or accept minor to major risk in other investments—all of which may or may not be worth the amount of tax savings they provide. The tax estimates help you determine these values and their effects.

## The Checklist

You should create a checklist of things you will need to do to complete a certain phase of your financial plan. The checklist enumerates various tasks that must be completed by certain dates. The financial planner will assist you in determining and completing each task.

Some typical items on a list of recommendations might be:

| PRIORITY | TARGET DATE | COMPLETION DATE |
|---|---|---|
| 1. Draft will | | |
| 2. Draft will with trust | | |
| 3. Review will | | |
| 4. Increase life insurance to | | |
| 5. Adjust type of life insurance | | |
| 6. Update health and major medical insurance | | |

| PRIORITY | TARGET DATE | COMPLETION DATE |
|---|---|---|
| 7. Take out disability insurance | | |
| 8. Increase homeowners' or tenants' dwelling insurance | | |
| 9. Increase homeowners' or tenants' liability | | |
| 10. Increase homeowners' or tenants' replacement cost on contents | | |
| 11. Increase auto liability and uninsured motorist to | | |
| 12. Take out personal liability policy (umbrella) | | |
| 13. Release equity in home | | |
| 14. Reduce taxes by making investments in current year | | |

These and many, many more condensed ideas are offered only after all the facts are known and the "what if" calculations have been computed in an attempt to predict their results.

## Disclosure Form

At the end of the financial plan, a written statement should be made available by the planner that discloses any potential conflict of interest. The potential conflict occurs because the planner who recommends investments may also receive brokerage fees for investing your money. The statement will inform you of the straight fee for the financial services and if that fee includes investment services. If you paid a flat fee for the financial plan, you can take that plan and do what you wish with it. You can stick it in a drawer somewhere, or you can carry out the recommendations. Moreover, if you carry out the plan you don't have to use the brokerage services of the planner. However, if you feel this person has integrity, the financial planner who prepared the plan is the most qualified person to invest your money and maintain your accounts.

The main point of having a disclosure statement should be to inform you that the preparer of the plan who advises you on investments might also receive commissions and fees if he invests your money for you. Not all financial planners are brokers; many are, and there is nothing wrong with this. If it weren't for the better brokers and financial planners, most people would never consider financial planning at all!

**PART III**

# THE BASICS: WHAT YOU NEED TO KNOW ABOUT MONEY

*or*

*"USEFUL TOOLS AND HIDDEN TREASURES"*

Hearst Castle, CA

# I
# A FEW BASICS
# IN GENERAL

A few basic principles of and concepts about money will help you understand and put into perspective the information you gather in order to begin on the road to riches.

## Saving

Because you need money in order to make money, the road to wealth starts off with saving. Unless you receive an inheritance or rob a bank, you must save money to accumulate it.

Saving takes determination and discipline because you have to reduce personal expenses in order to free up the money to save. All of us have expensive tastes, but we can cut back. We can go out to dinner less, see fewer movies or go to matinees; cut down on the use of plastic money or pay the "plastic" bills immediately to avoid high interest rates; bypass purchasing a second or third television set, a second refrigerator, or a new car every four years. These expenses provide only marginal benefits for a short period of time while consuming hard-earned dollars and offering no monetary returns. Use the money to invest instead.

If you do not reduce your expenses, if you do not discipline yourself, you can forget about achieving your financial goals. Money does not appear magically, and your financial goals will not be met by just wishing them to come true.

It is important to start your program immediately because the longer you allow your money to grow, the greater it will grow through the "magic" of compounding. Starting early also allows you to choose lower-risk investments. A person in his twenties can put away a small sum of money in low-risk investments, accept a lower rate of return, and still have a large nest egg to retire on. On the other hand, someone who starts saving in his fifties must incur greater risks in trying to make enough to retire on. Take action! The best day to start your investment program was yesterday; the second best day is today.

## Money and Time

Another key to financial success is your optimum use of time in relationship to money. Think of time as an investment, and analyze its uses.

When investing your time, consider how you can enhance your future financial position. A job will bring in income, but if you allocate time to reading papers, books, magazines in order to gather as many ideas as possible, you will develop a base for assessing your opportunities, whether they relate to an employer's offer, a partner's view, an advisor's opinion, a friend's counsel, or a salesperson's pitch.

Much can be learned when inputting the concept of time into the results of an investment.

If you invested $1,000 at an 8% rate of return for a five-year period, the ending value would be $1,469. Yet, if you wait just another five years, the value would be $2,159—a more than one-and-a-half-times increase.

For those who have large amounts of money, consider the following: If you invested $10,000,

| Number of years | Rate of return | Result |
|:---:|:---:|:---:|
| 3 | 10% | $ 13,310 |
| 5 | 10% | $ 16,105 |
| 10 | 10% | $ 25,937 |
| 25 | 10% | $108,347 |

Obviously time is on your side and you are much better off putting as much money as possible, as often as possible, and as soon as possible to work for you.

Another major consideration is the time factor combined with the percentage return: If you invested $1,000 and earned 8% interest for 20 years, your account would be worth $4,661. Compare this to the same time period of 20 years but a 9% interest rate—an ending value of $5,604, more than a thousand dollars difference. As you can see, one percent difference in earnings can mean over 20% in ending value. A 12% rate of return over 20 years yields an ending value of $9,646—a dramatic increase in ending balance.

As you can see, the higher the rate of return and the more time you have, the greater the ending value of your investment.

## Leverage—The Use of Other People's Money

To borrow or not to borrow! That is the classic financial question—

whether it is better to shun the perils of borrowing or to use other people's money (OPM).

Borrowing means using OPM which is usually obtained through a bank or other financial institution. A lever is used to lift one or more objects that normally cannot be moved. Financial leverage lets you purchase things you normally could not buy. Should you leverage your assets to achieve financial success?

The answer, of course, depends on the individual.

For instance, you would be hard pressed to pay cash for a $100,000 house, but you could pay a down payment of $10,000 and borrow the rest. If you later sold the house for $110,000, your profit would be 10% of the total purchase price of $100,000. However, you only paid $10,000 out of pocket. Therefore, you would make a 100% return on your money. This is a good example of using OPM for your own benefit. (The reverse is true, of course: if the house drops in value or is destroyed by fire without homeowners' insurance, you are still responsible for the loan balance.)

In general, it is better to pay cash for most items if you can afford to. The rule of thumb is to borrow 1) if it helps increase your productivity; 2) if the cost is substantially reduced by tax benefits; or 3) if the item purchased with borrowed funds will appreciate in value.

## Inflation

When investing for future return, the most common fear which many knowledgeable investors have is fear of inflation. Why, you ask yourself, should you be concerned with what is often termed "the silent assault"?

Most of us think of inflation as an overall increase in consumer prices, thus damaging the purchasing ability of those who have fixed income and fixed investments. While this is true, there are other areas which can be affected much more critically than we realize. Even in times of recession, many areas of the economy tend to increase in value and in cost: automobiles, houses, offices, and appliances. A very basic protection against inflation is to own these assets which tend to increase in price and value each year.

In short, inflation eats away at the spending value of your money. To illustrate:

In the chart below, when the dollar value falls behind inflation, if any one of the listed inflation rates occurs, the purchasing power of

$1,000 will be reduced to:

| Number of years | Inflation rate of | | |
|---|---|---|---|
| | 2% | 4% | 8% |
| 5 | $905.73 | $821.93 | $680.58 |
| 10 | $820.35 | $675.56 | $463.19 |
| 15 | $743.01 | $555.26 | $315.24 |
| 20 | $672.97 | $456.39 | $214.55 |

Thus in 20 years, at an inflation rate of 8%, $1,000 will lose 80% of its purchasing power; or the $1,000 you hold in your hand today, if not properly invested, will buy only $202.97 in goods and services in 20 years.

Another way to view this process is to see how much money it will take in the future to buy today's $1,000 of goods and services:

| Number of years | Inflation rate of | | |
|---|---|---|---|
| | 2% | 4% | 8% |
| 5 | $1,104.08 | $1,216.65 | $1,469.33 |
| 10 | $1,218.99 | $1,480.24 | $1,469.33 |
| 15 | $1,345.87 | $1,800.94 | $3,172.17 |
| 20 | $1,485.92 | $2,191.12 | $4,660.96 |

As previously mentioned, inflation can work in your favor by your investing in those items which you believe will appreciate the most. However, when you plan your investment program, make sure that the investments you purchase will stand on their own merits regardless of the inflationary trend. During periods of inflation, almost any asset or investment tends to do well and can therefore be misleadingly "safe." The actual structure of the investment is of primary importance: Is it sound?

There are many possible investments which will hedge against inflation. All should be closely scrutinized. Collectible items (coins, paintings) do quite well over the years but are not very liquid, do not produce monthly income, and seldom have any tax benefit. Stocks tend to rise in value with inflation on an overall basis.

Which brings us back to:

## Inflation—A Worthwhile Reason to Borrow?

Borrowing money for investments that produce multiple benefits, future inflation protection, and various tax write-offs can be extremely beneficial. However, if the assets are purchased prematurely or inappropriately, dangerous financial problems can result.

We have already discussed one of the most popular inflation hedges: the purchase of real estate. As the demand increases, so will its value. Real estate prices keep up with inflation rates.

Like borrowing to buy real estate, "buying on margin" in the stock market can be profitable. An individual who is extremely confident that a particular stock will go up in value might put up a certain amount of money to buy the stock and actually be able to use other dollars to purchase more stock by borrowing for short periods of time. The potential for profit must be weighed against its reverse, however. If a stock that the individual borrowed money to purchase actually declines in value, he or she not only loses the original capital but is now on the hook for the additional money borrowed.

In general, short-term consumer loans do not let the borrower take advantage of the effects of inflation because the life of the loan is too short for inflation to take effect. In fact, short-term consumer loans end the financial lives of thousands each year. Because people are encouraged to charge more purchases than they can afford at the highest interest rates, their owed balance continues to grow like an uncontrolled wildfire.

On the other hand, inflation is a powerful ally for the long-term borrower. As inflation erodes the purchasing power of the dollar, the price of goods and services and the wages you earn are adjusted upward for inflation, but the payment you owe on the loan stays the same.

## Risk:Reward

The phrase—and concept—"risk:reward" really does exist.

A governing principle of investments is the risk:reward relationship. Simply put, the greater the potential reward, the greater the risk and vice versa. You can look at this in two ways: the greater gain you seek, the more risk you must assume; or the greater the safety you seek, the lower return you will receive.

The principle of risk:reward applies to all investments. The level of risk is usually determined by the unknown certainty of future value. The present value of an investment or business may not be substantial, but if some day this same business produces great dividends, its market value will greatly increase. Risk factors include an investment's lack of popularity; a growth potential based on changes in the economy that polarize investors; the holding on to a particular stock with hopes of its producing high dividends in the future, thus inflating its price far in excess of its actual value. Many times it is this anticipation that affects investment values (others are the actual demand for use, such as real estate; and consumption, such as wheat and grain).

Risk can be reduced by following the most conservative path. For example, if establishing a new business, one can research extensively the pros and cons of its success, avoid extensive borrowing, and be patient in expecting long-term results. Purchasing real estate can be accomplished conservatively by avoiding borrowing funds; for those few people who can afford a cash purchase, safety exists in that they owe no one a mortgage and don't have the potential of foreclosure by a bank.

Dollar-cost averaging can reduce risk when investing in the stock market. No one alive or dead has ever been able to pinpoint exact highs and lows in the stock market every time. Dollar-cost averaging means you invest equal sums of money at set intervals over a period of time. By investing a fixed sum of money regularly, you end up buying more shares when the price of the stock is low and fewer shares when the price is high.

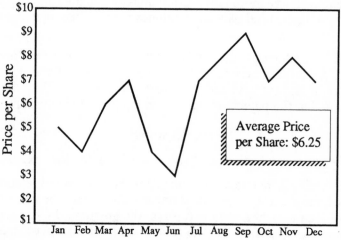

Monthly Stock Purchase of $100

Dollar-cost averaging lessens the "penalty" of not buying at the lowest price and therefore lessens the need to have perfect timing. For the investor who does not have the time to spend watching over his stocks, dollar-cost averaging is the way to go.

# Defensive Planning

Regardless of your investment strategy, you should always maintain an adequate cash reserve. The importance of maintaining a cash reserve is obvious. You need to put away something so that when an emergency—or opportunity—occurs you can get to your money quickly.

A cash reserve is necessary not only to take care of an emergency, but also to ensure that you stick to your long-range financial plan. Investments such as real estate partnerships, oil income funds, and tax shelters require years for the accrual of full benefits. Relying on stocks and bonds for an emergency fund could force you to liquidate them at an untimely or awkward time. For long-term bank deposits there is the proverbial "substantial penalty for early withdrawal." A cash reserve allows you the luxury of ensuring that your long-term investments stay long term. A cash reserve lets you determine when to buy and sell your various assets; an emergency will not force your hand. In fact, it is wise to have a large cash reserve so if a great investment opportunity comes along you can invest by using your cash reserve. This is known as defensive planning.

Defensive planning should be the first priority of a financial plan. Knowing that you can handle any financial crisis will add to your peace of mind. Once you are sure you can handle any contingency, you can begin to invest as aggressively as you like. By having a cash reserve as your investment foundation, you will be able to take a loss without fear of financial failure. Defensive planning allows you to control the size, type, and timing of your investments because you can commit your funds knowing you will not have to pull out of them in an emergency. Your investment decisions will not be clouded by the shadow of a potential crisis. A cash reserve will allow you to sleep better at night knowing that you have not gone in over your head.

# Diversification

Diversification is another old principle, the practice of which adds safety to your investment activities. It is said that Chinese merchants in ancient times loaded portions of their wares on different ships. If one ship sank, the merchant lost only a part of his wares. If the merchant put all of his wares on one ship and it sank, he faced financial disaster. The merchant diversified his assets so that if something went wrong with one ship, he could still continue his trade.

This practice should apply to your investing. Each investor should put his assets in various investment vehicles so that if one investment vehicle is struck by disaster the whole portfolio will not go down with it.

You can have this done for you by investing in a stock mutual fund which holds dozens of stocks from different industries. If you invest on your own, do not buy stocks from the same industry. For instance, if you think the automobile industry will do well, do not buy both GM and Chrysler. If you do and some unanticipated disaster occurs, your ship will sink. Find other sectors or industries completely different from the automobile industry to invest into—paper products, gold mining, food companies. The point is: No matter how good an investment looks or how safe it may seem, do not put all of your wares on the same ship. Diversify!

## A Few Words of Caution

### LENDING TO A FRIEND

Never—I repeat, never—lend to a friend or relative with the expectation of being paid back. You may think this policy is rude and uncaring, but consider all the horror stories about best friends who entered into a loan and parted enemies.

However, if you cannot resist before you do make a loan, think about what you will do when the time comes to repay the loan and it is not repaid. Can you afford to let your future be damaged by faulty loans or lost friendships? Can you afford to consider the transaction as a gift?

The bottom line is only lend money that you are willing and able to give as a gift and consider repayment as an unexpected bonus if it occurs.

### BANKRUPTCY

If you are having financial difficulties, take time to figure out all angles before giving up. Some people advise going into bankruptcy, but this action should not be taken lightly. Bankruptcy remains on your credit references for years. It also damages your reputation. How many people who have been burned by a bankrupt individual will do business with that individual again?

### BEWARE:IMPULSES AND HOT TIPS

Many Americans suffer from an attitude of negativism. They fail to invest in projects and programs that, if successful, could greatly benefit them. I have heard more stories than I care to recall about persons who passed up investment opportunities because they were not willing to take a chance. These people do not believe in the future. They will usually work for someone else during their lifetimes only to discover at retirement that their funds and retirement income are not sufficient to keep pace with inflation. Had these people acted on just one of the many opportunities that passed them by, they would be financially comfortable in their retirement.

For those people who possess a positive attitude and are willing and eager to take chances, careful analysis of just what they are getting into is necessary. Future potential for profits is usually unknown. Some investments that appear to be risky turn out to be quite profitable, others not so profitable. Some opportunities that cross our paths will never be profitable for reasons of structure, timing, suitability, legality.

*Beware hot tips and someone else's impulses.* You must be fully aware of everything you are getting into. Research to ensure you are not making any undue mistakes. Hot tips have turned many an investor's attitude into a cold iceberg. I often wonder why if an investment idea is so great people are trying to get me to invest in it? Why not keep it for themselves? Invest in facts, not hot tips! Only you will watch out for your money.

Look at the success of the individual who is giving the advice. Don't be fooled by rented offices, leased automobiles, and fancy jewelry. I have seen some pretty wealthy looking people who were in a fancy office one day and the next day were filing for bankruptcy. Remember, wealth is not always visible by appearance. A person can't wear a million dollars, but he can wear a few thousand dollars and lease a fancy office and a luxury car. If you need help, find someone who is familiar with the investment you are interested in. If you are purchasing an investment through a broker, find a broker others have worked with favorably.

Be very wary of any investment or broker that requires you invest within a set period of time. Even though a few investments that cross our paths are unusually good opportunities and require an on-the-spot decision, for most of us, they should be avoided unless we are extremely qualified in the particular field. If you rely on someone else to help you make a decision, be sure that someone has no financial interest in your decision.

It is my opinion that only the person who is an expert in a particular field of investments is qualified to act quickly. Only he can see the untapped investment resource. The rest of us should proceed with caution. Usually the investment that requires your dollars immediately is based on the seller's need or desire to acquire your money on an impulse. This pressure requires you to make a decision. Many people who are under pressure will give way to this pressure in order to get out of an uncomfortable situation, such as dealing with a high-pressure salesperson. A good idea is to tell the selling person that you never make a decision the first day; you must think about it. Or you can leave your checkbook at home so you can't be talked into something you don't want to do.

Also, beware of those who tout inside information, especially brokers of securities. There are certain securities' laws and regulations that prohibit brokers from giving out inside or non-public information about investments. Any substantial information that would affect an investor or potential investor's buy or sell transactions must be made public for all to share. If your broker gives you inside information, he or she is either exaggerating or actually breaking the law. If you are found guilty of making profits from inside, non-public information, you may be subject to criminal charges, not to mention fines and return of any profits made.

Caution must be exercised against impulse even in a "sure"—legal and tested—investment. Even though your friends have made large profits, you may not be suited for an investment that suits others. The suitability of an investment for you is the primary element that will allow success or set up for failure.

Most investments that the average person should consider are long-term growth vehicles, carefully researched. You are an easy mark for deception and pressure by people wanting your money if you appear anxious and uneducated. It is wise to begin planning weeks, if not months, before investing. You can then re-evaluate your decision before you actually commit yourself. There's no hurry. It probably took you years to make your money. A few more days won't matter.
you years to make your money. A few more days won't matter.

# II

# THE SPECIFICS OF INVESTING

The most important task when investing is determining which type of investment is suitable for your needs. Years ago it was easy for a person to know where to invest extra capital. The choices were to invest into the family business, purchase land, buy government bonds, or, with some knowledge and contacts, invest in the stock market. Choosing the investment was simple. Government bonds were backed by the U.S. government and therefore safe. Real estate pretty much held its own if you could pay the taxes and keep up with the financing. The stock exchange offered a little risk and a chance for great returns.

Times have changed. The investment world is no longer quite so simple.

Two basic principles of investing will help you begin your investing career:

1. *Know your market!* Do all the research possible before investing! Even if you are putting all your faith in an advisor, you should have some understanding of the risk involved. After all, it's your financial future that these investments are going to affect. You need to understand the investment and the market in which the investment is sold. You need to take the time to learn exactly how the desired investment is structured and to categorize the investment at its appropriate level of risks and features. Others will try to advise you about what to do and where to invest. You should never—I repeat, never—make any changes or invest until you have done the necessary research and analysis required for that particular decision.

The more volatile the market value of the investment the more you should know about its makeup. There is nothing more disappointing—or frightening—than owning an investment when the value is down and not having the experience and knowledge to maintain confidence that it will make a comeback. If you don't understand the market, it will be impossible to stay in the forefront of profit. If you do understand the market, you will be able to choose those investments that will work to your advantage.

Investing is a necessary activity if you are ever going to reach your goal of becoming a millionaire. Whether you invest into your own business or that of others by way of investment programs, you must be very careful. I don't mean that being careful precludes you from taking high risk for high return. What I am pointing out is that the more you know about an investment, the higher the odds of success you can place into your favor.

2. *Contrarian Theory.* This is a technique that thousands of successful investors have used since the beginning of time. Simply put: Buy those investments that others are not interested in, that they are willing to let go of to buyers, like you, who later profit from an increasing market value. This practice does not have to include a large amount of risk. For example, in real estate, if investing in a home, you are going to need shelter from the weather anyway, and if you are investing when others are saying that the market is down and therefore prices are low, what better time to buy. The catch? You must be willing to hang on to an investment that is not in its peak market.

Most every investment will deal with timing and fads. For example: Suppose you wanted to begin a retail business specializing in gold jewelry. At this particular time, you are not ready to set up the store but would like to begin buying the supplies so when you open your doors you will be fully stocked with the necessary materials. Well, would you like to buy your supplies of gold while the prices are high or low? Of course, you would like to buy your supplies when the market is low. That means that you will be stocking up with supplies when the demand for gold jewelry is down. Then, hopefully, when you are ready to set up shop, the demand for gold jewelry will be higher than when you started buying. If it is not, then you should wait to open until the demand is more in your favor.

This type of practice is similar to the contrarian theory. Those who can buy when an investment is down take the risks of a non-recovery and wait until the market is positioned in their favor in order to profit quite handsomely.

I am not saying that every investment that is down will regain its value. However, it is this uncertainty that makes other investors give in and give up future profits. If you need or like the investment that is unpopular and can afford the time and funds to wait, you may find that some day many dollars end up in your bank account.

Yes, but what *is* a good investment? Often I am asked this question. I am afraid that I have to answer a question with more questions: What do you want your money to do? How safe do you want it to be? Do you need it to produce income? Do you need tax benefits from it? Do you need the investment to be liquid?

As you can see, and as stated earlier, to determine the right investment, you must first determine what need to fill. It is like the child's toy that requires the child to place the proper pegs in the proper holes. You must place a square peg in a square hole, a round peg in a round hole, and so on. In this example,

The hole is the void or need you have to fill.

The investment is the shaped peg you will fill the hole (need) with.

The square peg might represent the need for maximum safety. The choices for this need might be filled by T-bills, certificates of deposits, insured savings accounts, and government bonds.

The round peg might represent the need for income. This might be satisfied by various insured savings accounts, government bonds, preferred stocks, debentures, rental income from real estate, oil royalty funds, etc. All produce income.

The octagon peg might represent the desire for tax-free income. This kind of income-producing investment might be municipal bonds or other tax-sheltered investment programs which shelter income by providing additional tax benefits.

The star-shaped peg might represent the need for tax-deductible benefits. These benefits might come by way of real estate properties or limited partnership investments in real estate, oil R & D, cattle, energy leasing, etc. All will offset or shelter income from other investment income.

The triangle may indicate growth potential. These investments concentrate strictly on growth—not safety, income, tax benefits, or liquidity. These might be various common stocks, leveraged real estate, oil drilling and cattle breeding programs, etc.

As you can see, each category of investments has its own features. Some have tax benefits but are not liquid. Some produce very reliable income but don't protect us from inflation.

So what is the best investment? Once you determine the need, you can begin to search out what type of investment to use and then in what specific investment or company to invest.

## The Stock Market

Wall Street may seem like a strange and mysterious place, but for those who understand it, Wall Street can be a place where profits—and fortunes—are made. It is not difficult to become a competent stock investor. All it takes is a little time. The noted economist, John Maynard Keynes, only spent 10 minutes each day on his stock portfolio and amassed a large fortune.

Understanding a few basic principles helps too.

While there are many methods and systems in the stock market, most have only a brief period of success—if any. Even the old maxim of buying the stock of a good company and holding it for decades no longer holds true. Ben Graham, the originator of the "buy 'em and forget 'em" concept in his classic tome, *Securities Analysis*, was right for his era, the 30s through the 60s, but he would have lost his money in the high inflation and turbulent market of the 70s.

When investing in stocks and bonds, one of the first realities is that you must be willing to sell when you feel you have made enough profit. Many people are excited to find that a particular stock has risen substantially in price and then lose those profits by hanging on too long because the stock experiences a decline from its prior high. You cannot be too greedy or wait too long. Profits in the market are made off those who have been caught unprepared. Brokers get paid when you buy or sell, regardless of the money you have made or lost. Some may try to keep you trading just to improve their income.

The basic idea of buying stocks of sound companies currently in disfavor still applies—as long as you do not hold them for decades. Buy the stocks that are currently out of favor with the market and sell them at the peak of market frenzy. This pattern usually follows the economic cycle which lasts about four years. Buying and selling every few years enables you to take advantage of peaks and valleys in the price of the stock so you can maximize your profits. The strategy is simple: sell high and buy low. But you must have the stomach for it. Usually, at the peak in the market, everyone is euphoric, and selling requires courage. Buying when everyone is selling requires courage. Buying when everyone is preaching doom and gloom takes nerves of steel.

Even if you have a strong stomach, you must have common sense and wait for the market to tell you what to do. Here are a few ways to predict the major turning points in the market:

1. At major turning points, usually a major financial publication will have a headline article on how the current trend will continue for the foreseeable future. In August, 1982, one business magazine cover story headlined, "Is the Market Dead?" Subsequently, the stock market had the greatest rally (increase) in its history.

2. The number of stocks that reach yearly highs and lows can be a very good indicator. If the highs outnumber the lows by a wide margin— say 400:1—the market has peaked, and it is time to get out.

3. Another way to tell if the market has reached its peak is a flood of new issues which are eagerly gobbled up by the public. Usually there will be articles in the press highlighting this fact.

These are just a few of the ways to tell if a major turning point is at hand. With research, you can find many other ways to confirm major trends.

For the average individual who wants to avoid losing money in the stock market, a mature attitude should be taken when investing:

*Step 1.* Find a stock or mutual fund you feel very comfortable with based on reliable information and common sense. Avoid using "hot tips" because by the time you hear them, many others may have been warmed by the fire and you may be left with cold ashes.

*Step 2.* Determine how much money on an initial investment you are willing to commit. At that point, only invest 60% of those dollars in your first transaction, maintaining a 40% back-up fund. Continually analyze your investment to determine if you are still happy with the original decision. If your investment suddenly drops for some unfortunate reason, you can defensively invest another 20%. Knowing that you achieved an even better price-per-share buy on the second purchase can help ease disappointment. On the other hand, if the stock goes up, you can look for comparable stock that will duplicate your success and add diversification or re-invest in your original program. The final 20% can be invested some time in the future when general market trends force this same stock down for a short period of time. This method, like many others, does not guarantee investment success and is only meant for the average investor. The strategy behind it is only to prevent risking all of your capital on one investment transaction.

A more favorable investment tactic for the average person who hopes to accumulate money for retirement on a conservative basis is that of dollar-cost averaging. Here you make monthly or quarterly purchases of a particular stock or mutual fund, a buying technique which allows you to continually buy at a slightly better-than-average price.

And a few common-sense rules will help you think "stock market":

1. Be a contrarian. Buy low and sell high.

2. Don't buy into hot tips or fads. By the time you hear about

them, most of the gains have already been made.

3. Don't chase stocks. If the price moves away from you, then find another stock that is within reach.

4. Cut your losses. Don't let the losses grow and grow thinking that in order to break even you will sell when the stock comes back.

5. Don't marry your stocks. Just because they have been good to you in the past doesn't mean they will continue to perform well. Don't become sentimental. A stock doesn't care if you love it or not—or own it or not.

6. Don't buy a stock based on one new development or new product. Usually it has already been discounted by the market. When the product is officially announced by the company, the price of the stock is unaffected or, as is more often the case, the price will fall.

By combining a few simple rules, common sense, a strong stomach, and patience, you too can prosper in the stock market.

## Stocks and Bonds and Mutual Funds

For those of you who are interested in having investments for long-term growth and/or income and/or liquidity if needed, stocks offer some very rewarding opportunities if placed properly in an investment portfolio. For example, most blue chip stocks are very well known, provide little risk, but also little reward, in potential stock price increases. These stocks are primarily purchased for extra income with minimum expectations that the stocks will increase in value. On the other side of the spectrum, if stock is purchased from aggressive companies whose stock tends to be very volatile in the market, profound gains can be amassed in a good or "bull" market. However, these stocks can also provide major losses during a poor or "bear" market.

In general, income which conservative stocks can provide can be just as easily obtained in the money market area where there is more liquidity and safety of principal. Rather than investing in conservative income stocks, it might be advisable to earn your investment income from various other assets and take a more aggressive stance in the stock market with fewer dollars, leaving those other dollars to be secured in cash positions. Taking this type of position may increase your chances for appreciation in the market with fewer dollars at risk.

One market opportunity is the new-issue market. Here, a business that is incorporated and wants to raise money for operations will sell stock and issue stock certificates for the first time. The thing to consider in this kind of stock is that unless the country is waiting for the company to go public, the stock could drop after being issued.

Generally, buying and selling individual stocks on the stock market is not a good plan for inexperienced investors. A better investment might be in mutual funds which allow the investor the opportunity to be involved in a group investment program that employs a professional manager to buy and sell individual stocks. The concept of a mutual fund is that the average investor who does not have the knowledge or the time to pick and choose specific stocks can have someone do it for him.

When investing in a mutual fund, you need to consider exactly what stocks and bonds the fund is allowed to purchase and review the fund's track record. The bottom line here is that you look for a fund whose management has a good reputation for protecting investors during volatile markets and making wise decisions with money. Remember that the mutual fund is only as good as the stocks or bonds within it and the managers who manage it.

## Oil and Gas

Oil and gas is essential to a modern industrial nation. Without it, the world's economy would come to a halt. Presently, the U.S. is at the mercy of foreign powers for a large part of its oil supply. Although there are other energy sources available, most are impractical, costly, or experimental. Oil and gas, even with hefty price increases, remain cheap and efficient sources of energy. It appears the U.S. will continue to rely on them for its energy needs in the foreseeable future. For those people with staying power, oil and gas can prove to be very profitable.

Oil has been called "black gold," but until recently, in order to make money in the oil market, you had to own stocks, own the land, be an independent wildcatter, or own an oil company. Now an individual can buy commodity futures and options or become a direct owner by purchasing units in one of the many oil and gas limited partnerships (see additional discussion on limited partnerships in Chapter IV). Considering the uncertainty of future oil supplies, some participation in the oil and gas industry, as a balance to other investments within your investment portfolio, might be considered.

*Oil drilling programs*-limited partnerships that invest your money into drilling for oil and gas, are high risk but also high profit if successful.

*Income or royalty funds*–more conservative programs, purchase the oil and gas, after it is found, from those who have already taken all the risks. Here the risk does not lie in the actual search for the resource, but in its resale. If the price of oil and gas decreases after the resource is purchased, your profits decline. If the price of oil and gas increases, so does the profit of the investment fund and eventually your share of the partnership.

## Tangibles

For many people tangibles can be a very satisfying investment. Tangibles are investments which you can touch and see, such as paintings, jewelry, sculpture, coins, stamps, comic books, and even antique automobiles. Their accumulation poses storage problems and potential losses from damage or theft. However, they can offer greater personal satisfaction than a piece of paper such as a stock certificate.

Tangibles require a serious commitment from the investor. They are not easily liquidated and usually incur a fairly high commission or brokerage fee. It is best if you choose to invest in an area you already know about. If not, it should be thoroughly researched. You should also examine your emotional commitment. Will you be willing to sell when the time ˙comes? If you are not willing to sell, then you should not consider it an investment. For the patient and knowledgeable, tangibles can be both profitable and enjoyable.

## Cash and Cash Equivalents

When dealing with T-bills issued by the U.S. government, various C.D.s issued by banks, and other investments with a relatively safe cash position, you need to have a basic knowledge of the risk involved in holding such an asset. First, determine how long your money will be tied up. Find out whether or not there are any early withdrawal penalties and calculate exactly what they will be if you need to cash out prematurely. Next, determine why you have chosen to stay in a cash position and realize that although you may like the idea of earning interest every day, you are placing yourself at risk—risk of potential tax consequences and lack of growth due to inflation. You need a healthy cash reserve, but realize that due to inflation these monies will remain idle.

## Investment Debriefing

Let me insert here repeated words of advice: When you have acquired some excess cash, invest wisely. Don't fall for get-rich-quick schemes; they never work. Such investment vehicles will not allow you to sleep at night without worrying. Invest in things that you understand. Make sure you are comfortable with your investments. Don't be pressured into something you do not like. Many investments are complex, especially those that deal in taxes. Have it explained to you and then explained again. If you do not feel comfortable, don't do it. Often times common sense and gut instincts are better than financial prose.

I have touched quite briefly on just a few very basic investment opportunities available. The following chapters deal with additional investment opportunities. Specific, detailed descriptions of investments can be found in Appendix B.

# III

# THE SPECIFICS OF REAL ESTATE

The U.S., the land of opportunity!

Some people scoff at this idea complaining that opportunities in the U.S. died out with the settling of the west. At that time, the railroad companies were offering free land where they laid track in order to create communities that would some day become dependent upon railroad services, thus creating a consumer base for their mode of transportation. No doubt those families that accepted the challenge of establishing a new frontier and moved west now control some of the largest bank accounts in the western states today.

Opportunities in real estate continue to thrive. If you take a look at foreign countries, you will see that having the right to purchase land is one of the greatest opportunities that this country still offers. The average European will most likely live out his life in a very small flat or apartment and never enjoy the freedom of owning buildings and land and creating wealth. In the third world countries, such as South America or Africa, the major distinction between wealth and poverty is the ability of a few families to own land and control the lives of others. The U.S. still remains, for the average individual, one of the final frontiers of "staking a claim" to future prosperity.

Due to various economic changes, a great many obstacles arise in buying real estate. These obstacles might be final signs of a changing economy which may take this great opportunity away from many of us forever if we don't act now.

Time, income, cash reserves, desire, patience, and knowledge are some of the resources you will need in order to be successful in purchasing real estate. You don't necessarily need to have any more than one or two of these resources to be successful. Let us look at just what we mean.

*Time.* This is probably one of the most valuable assets you possess. The longer you have to acquire any asset the less you are required to sacrifice in the present. If you can afford 30 years to pay off a fixed amount on a mortgage loan, each payment will be less. Obviously, then, the younger you are the more advantage you have. If you are starting later in life, you may have to increase the monthly payments by taking out a 10-, 15-, or 20-year loan.

*Income.* If you, or possibly a spouse, have a consistent income that can always be counted on, buying real estate becomes relatively easy. Even for the successful real estate speculator, the mortgage payment must go on.

*Cash reserves.* If you do not have a predictable monthly income, a large cash reserve can help you through any short months. Also, large cash offers, when buying real estate, can many times provide the opportunity for successful negotiations.

*Desire.* One must have the true desire to succeed, for the road to success is many times very rocky and hard. Those who aspire to reach their destination will soon achieve success.

*Patience* is a great part of an investor's personality. This is especially true of the real estate investor. Real estate properties are long-term commitments, usually for retirement assets.

*Knowledge.* This is probably the most powerful tool you can have as an investor in any commodity. Having the ability to make intelligent decisions will allow you to turn ideas into profits. Knowing the ropes adds protection against poor decisions and provides insight to more profitable experiences.

When investing in real estate, you need to learn the basics of real estate as a whole. Learn about how properties become available and what to avoid. Learn all you can about types of financing you will commit yourself to. Attending real estate classes from more than one instructor is advisable because there are many different methods of buying and selling. Look for the method that will allow you to maintain a happy ownership position regardless of where the economy goes. Inflation will continue to affect this country's economy, but you should never depend on an increase in value of your property to get you out of a tight situation. Inflation can help all of us who own real estate; however, it may disappoint those who expect its assistance.

Real estate over the years has been a good investment for most people. In some cases people have made millions just buying and selling properties. However, buyer, beware! Any investment should be considered on an individual basis. What is right for you and your family? Should you even consider real estate at all?

## Personal Residence

The most basic purchase of real estate is your personal residence. If it requires an additional moonlighting job or taking in boarders or roommates, you should seriously consider making this investment above all others unless your present circumstances preclude your doing so. I have seen many individuals who procrastinated in making the necessary real estate investments end up paying the price of high rent and additional expenses later. I have seen people who have failed to make sacrifices in earlier years now pay more for government low-cost, subsidized rental apartments than they would be paying for a mortgage on homes that they put off buying not more than a few years ago. When prices and rents continue to rise, only those who own nothing will become slaves to inflation, and the gap between wealth and poverty will widen and forever diminish all hopes of living the good life.

But first—advice aside—*you* need to determine *your* need. Well, that seems obvious. You probably prefer a roof over your head—rain or shine. However, do you need a house or an apartment? Do you need to rent or buy?

The benefits of purchasing your own home are many. If you borrow the money to purchase the residence, most of the monthly mortgage payment will be interest cost which presently is fully tax deductible. Also deductible are your property taxes. The value of the residence may very well rise above original purchase price, a protection from inflation. If real estate prices go up, a phenomenon which increases rents, you do not have to pay more each month for housing; you agreed on a locked-in price at the time you purchased the mortgage. Not least of the positives is the pride of ownership.

The negatives? Well, if the real estate market is depressed with no signs of future growth, the economic benefit from buying is reduced; if the property's value goes down, you still have to pay the original loan balance off. Also, there are hidden costs in buying a home: closing costs which average $2,500 (not including the down payment); fire insurance and homeowners' protection; and maintenance. You are, after all, the sole protector of hearth and home: *You* repair the weathered siding, the missing shingles, the plumbing gone awry.

A more practical approach may clear up the debate of buying versus renting. What will your payment on a mortgage actually be?

If you are in a 28% tax bracket, 28% of every final dollar earned is paid out in taxes. You are left with 72% of that dollar for personal uses. However, if you spend a dollar on items that Congress and IRS are sympathetic to, such as mortgage interest and property tax, that dollar spent is deducted from your gross income. If your monthly house payment is, say, $1,200 per month and $1,000 goes to interest loan charges, that amount is tax deductible. Deducting this $1,000 interest charge from $1,000 of taxable earned income reveals:

$1,000 taxable income (normal tax $280)
$1,000 tax-deductible interest charge
—————
$   0 taxable income

Thus, by having the $1,000 interest deduction, we avoided paying $280 tax on our ordinary income. Our net mortgage payment then is actually $280 (tax savings) less than the original $1,200 or an after-tax cost of $920. For someone in a 15% tax bracket, the tax savings or net payment is not so beneficial.

The higher tax bracket you are in, the more advantageous tax deductions become and the more beneficial it is to buy real estate, especially if you get a good buy on the property in the first place and/or its value increases.

So, should you buy or rent? In general, if your house loan payments are not that much more than your rent and if real estate value appears to have great potential for appreciation, purchasing would be wise. However, if the net payment is much greater than renting and the real estate values do not appear to have the potential for appreciation, renting might be wiser until conditions improve.

Before buying, you need to become as familiar as possible with financial arrangements. Most of us are not in a position to buy for cash and will probably have to rely on some sort of financing.

The first financial consideration is how stable your income will be— regardless of how low the payments. Make sure that either you or your spouse has an extremely stable job or source of income. If your finances fluctuate, you will need to maintain a liquid emergency cash account. Serious problems can arise if you have a bad month and cannot pay the house payment. In fact, overextending is how many people lose their homes and provide good real estate buys for others.

There are two basic types of loans available, one is a fixed loan which provides for a predetermined fixed loan payment each month for a fixed number of years. The other is the variable loan, better known as the adjustable rate mortgage, ARM. Here the interest rate on the loan can fluctuate with the current interest rate. If interest rates rise, so do your payments. However, if rates reduce, you benefit.

There are several contingencies to consider when applying for a loan. Make sure you learn more about them. A few are: Is the loan fixed or variable? Can the loan be assumed by a new buyer who purchases your home? Are there prepayment penalties? What are the total costs of the loan? What are competitive rates and costs? To answer these questions, you should study the real estate loan market in your community.

And a word of caution: Be aggressive in your intentions, yet conservative in your actions.

1. Be very careful when attending seminars that talk about buying property with no money down. The technique may be possible, but offers great risks. One must be very familiar with all contingencies before becoming involved.

2. When looking for property, keep in mind your specific needs in housing: adequate space, neighborhood, ease of maintenance, yard size. What exactly do you need and expect from your living space?

3. Remodeling a residence to suit your needs can present problems: Costs are not directly tax deductible; costs can be excessive in time and money; some remodeling projects do *not* appreciate.

4. If, however, you have the time, expertise, and desire to fix up a property, the "do it yourself" method has built-in rewards. If you buy a depressed property in a nice area—the worst-looking house on the block—and bring it up to standard, you can watch its value rise to match the value of all other houses in the neighborhood. This is called "increasing equity." In fact, a general rule of thumb is to buy the least expensive home in a neighborhood because the more costly houses will automatically increase its value.

When sprucing up that house on the block which was left in ill repair before you bought it, keep a few things in mind. There will be various expenses involved. Usually this type of property will need landscaping, painting, and possible plumbing. Be prepared to do work, not to mention spend money. However, smart buyers make money by bringing the lower-valued property up to the value of the others on the block.

5. For people who have no inclination to fix and repair and do not have the time, multiple housing projects—condominiums and townhouses—are available. A self-maintenance crew will maintain the property for a fee, usually $50.00 a month. The condo offers a carefree ownership of property. However, because there are rules and regulations, opportunities to modify a property to enhance its resale value are almost non-existent. Also your property will always look like everyone else's, a similarity that causes more competition when selling. In most towns, a condo is not as marketable as a regular property.

## Rental Property

I personally feel that this type of real estate purchase is one of the most profitable arrangements in the long run, dollar-for-dollar invested, if you want to own a property but not maintain it on a day-to-day basis.

Because rental property requires certain occasional maintenance and improvements caused by misuse and wear and tear, Congress has given investors a tax break known as depreciation allowance. This allows you to claim a percentage of the value of your property as an investment loss, thus reducing your taxable income, even though the value of that property is actually increasing. You can only depreciate a rental property and not your home.

Another benefit is the increasing value of the property—if purchased in the right place and time.

These are the advantages. Some of the disadvantages?

The true price paid by the investor in rental properties runs the following gamut: a negative cash flow (falling short each month because rents received as a landlord don't make mortgage payments); additional legal liabilities assumed while holding rental property; additional costs for upkeep and maintenance; additional management and record-keeping hours lost to this type of ownership.

Not only can the managing and maintaining of the property be frustrating, but you are liable for what occurs on the property. If the tenant is injured or involved in a law suit, you most likely will be named in the suit as owner of the property. If the tenant doesn't pay the rent, you will probably have to hire an attorney to evict him. The tenant in turn may claim that you were unfair and sue you for discrimination or mismanagement of this most sacred castle, the tenant's home. Just try to evict a tenant on a timely basis. And, do you think that any person who refuses to pay rent on time will pay back rent after being evicted?

However, if you have a job with regular hours and have spare time to commit to other people's problems, then I firmly believe that in the long run you will prosper. Again, we must determine the structure of the investment intended and whether you fit the structure.

## Limited Partnerships

Those investors who do not choose to be landowners or landlords can invest in various limited partnerships which will provide as much or more growth as buying actual property.

Real estate investment trusts (REITs) and limited partnerships offer you direct participation in the profitability of real estate. Keep in mind that most all real estate ventures are based on long-term commitments, some as long as 10 years before the original investment plus profits materialize. However, most terms last from five to seven years. Any investment's appreciating takes time; and with real estate, if the project is sound, a very good appreciation rate will probably occur during the fourth or fifth year.

The partnerships do, however, require that you give up some of your profits in the partnership for commissions, management costs, and general expenses.

A bonus of REITs and partnerships is that you will incur no personal liability above and beyond the amount invested, and your time will never be intruded upon by various tenants making excessive demands.

Before becoming involved in a partnership of any kind, however, be sure that you are familiar with all of the basic features of the program. There are many good programs, and there are some bad ones. Look in various publications for the background, reputations, and track records of the people putting the partnership together, of the program itself. Also, check with your tax advisor: Will the particular real estate venture benefit your situation?

Real estate trusts and partnerships are discussed in more detail in IV.

# IV

# THE SPECIFICS OF TAXES AND TAX-SHELTERED INVESTMENTS

Although we never know what Congress will do from day to day regarding possible changes in our taxes, one thing is certain: Those who are working will support those who are not. Although this practice is humanitarian, it is not altogether fair, and the concern for most of us is where our taxes are being spent and how they can be reduced.

It is common knowledge that tax evasion is illegal, but tax avoidance is acceptable. There are many ways to reduce your taxes, but there are almost always strings attached.

## The Basic Tax Structure

Over the years, we have seen tax laws come and go, changing the investment behavior of the public. The laws are and always have been designed as tax breaks for certain interest groups that make up our economy. Some of these tax laws suppress or promote certain investment transactions, and you should become aware of them.

Keeping in mind that events and taxes will continually change, let us look at how the basic tax structure works.

### TAXABLE INCOME

There are three basic types of income for the average citizen. One is ordinary or earned income: the dollars you receive from your job, the taxable amount of income left after deductible expenses of your business. Another is investment income, those dollars earned from investments that you are actively involved with, including part-time businesses such as rental real estate properties. Last, there is passive income, dollars earned from investment vehicles such as stocks, money market funds, certificates of deposit, bonds, limited partnerships, etc. The passive income investments usually do not involve your time in active management.

Each different financial activity or investment transaction requires the filing of a special tax form. If you own a business, you will be required to complete a form called "Schedule C," a report of your gross income from sales or services minus various expenses incurred. The net figure, be it a profit or a loss, is reported as well on your regular tax form 1040. Income from passive investments necessitate forms for reporting taxable gains or losses. Investments which require your direct involvement like real estate rental properties also require a specific set of forms.

These three categories of income create certain challenges to the taxpayer who wants to reduce taxes. Some tax deductions are allowed to offset ordinary earned income while others are only allowed to offset portfolio or passive income. This is where the confusion sets in.

## TAX DEDUCTIONS

The higher the tax bracket you are in, the more beneficial tax deductions will be. But regardless of your present tax bracket, your planning should be influenced by the impact of taxes.

Tax deductions or tax write-offs are ways to reduce your tax bill. A write-off is nothing more than a tax-deductible expense. These deductions occur when various items are claimed as expenses for business or personal reasons.

In the area of earned income, certain excessive health care or moving expenses and employer expenses are deductible. However, the most significant tax deductions against ordinary earned income are the interest expense deduction on a home mortgage and retirement plans.

Business expenses include the cost of running a retail store or the expenses of a traveling salesperson. You need to know present tax laws that relate to you and your business to successfully "profit" from your expenses.

Deductions for participatory investments such as real estate rental properties remain available but with limitations. For example, the expenses incurred on loans can be deducted with limitations, and depreciation of a property may serve to offset ordinary income. The limitations differ from person to person and depend on the amount of total income earned and the number of rental properties owned.

A deduction for many individuals is the depreciation allowance. We are allowed to divide the value of an investment by its useful life and deduct that portion each year of the item's life. For example, a rental property worth $100,000 provides $3,333.33 of depreciable allowance per year for thirty years. This usually counts as a paper loss because most properties actually appreciate over time.

Obviously, you need to keep abreast of tax deductions that relate to your situation and provide up-to-date records of your expenses to your tax preparer in order to take advantage of all deduction possibilities.

Tax deductions reduce your tax bill, and legitimate deductions should be taken. However, it must be remembered that deductions are actual expenses. You must part with your money before you can claim a deduction. Do not create an expense or make a buying decision just because you can write off the purchase as an expense. Make sure your expenses are necessary. The deduction will only save a small portion of taxes. You do not get all of your money back at tax time. Tax deductions and expenses are deducted from your income, not from the taxes owed. Therefore, consider the actual economic benefits first and the tax breaks second.

Tax laws will always change. Make sure that you and your advisor keep in tune with the changes.

## Tax-Deferred Investments

You can reduce today's tax bill by deferring your income into the future through Individual Retirement Accounts, deferred savings plans with your employer, tax-deferred annuity plans, and institutional retirement funds. Tax-deferred savings and investment retirement funds allow an individual to side-track earned income from present taxable income while increasing retirement stability. The money and its accumulating interest are immune from taxes until withdrawn from the program.

The concept is simple—and highly advantageous to the investor. The retirement plan swings the present tax liability, which is probably high, out into the future—retirement—when the investor will probably be in a lower tax bracket. By avoiding taxes today and allowing the side-tracked funds to grow without stunting their growth by taxes, the end result can be absolutely astounding. Because of the time value of money, every dollar that is postponed from loss to taxes accelerates your acquisition of assets.

There are two types of annuity programs available to most Americans. One is the *Tax Sheltered Annuity (TSA),* which is an investment program offered by insurance companies for employees of non-profit organizations. The concept of the annuity is to give the investor a nest egg at retirement and supplement the investor's other retirement plans. The TSA program allows the investor to invest portions of his or her earned income into the annuity and actually deduct the same amount from taxable income. The TSA is only available to certain people with certain employers.

On the other hand, the *Tax Deferred Annuity (TDA)* is available to mostly anyone. Unlike the TSA, the dollars that go into the TDA investment are not deducted from earned income in the year invested, so no immediate tax saving occurs. However, the interest and/or profits from the investment remain sheltered from taxation until withdrawn from the plan.

When you establish a tax shelter, you can direct how the monies are invested in the plan. Some retirement plans restrict the investment decisions you can make because some employers hire investment advisors to manage the company's plan as a group program and you have little or no control. IRA, KEOGH, and pension profit-sharing plans, however, can be established at a bank or with an investment broker. The bank usually offers limited options, but the broker offers several. In the self-directed investment, you, the investor, are in control of where the actual assets of the plan are invested and can take on your own investment direction: cash, stocks, real estate, oil—you name it.

Most plans have restrictions, and you should know what the specific penalties and provisions are before you commit yourself to locking up your funds in any retirement fund. Even though saving for retirement is very important, because substantial penalties and taxes can occur, premature withdrawal of such funds might be a bigger mistake than not establishing the program in the first place.

One of the great advantages of these tax shelters is, of course, that they set into motion your retirement planning—a boring subject for some and a fearful reality for others. However, most plans will not allow you to withdraw funds without heavy penalties until you reach retirement age—unless you become legally disabled. Then you may withdraw funds to provide income. Thus, by building up your own retirement plan, you can reduce your income tax liability and accumulate an emergency disability fund—a self-made life insurance policy and a retirement program at the same time.

## Tax-Exempt Bonds

Interest earned on tax-exempt municipal bonds will be federal-tax free, and if the bonds are issued in the state in which you live, the interest may be state-tax free as well. However, this investment, like all others, is not without consequences. When you purchase a long-term bond, you must realize that it will not mature for many years, and during those years you will earn the contracted rate of interest. If interest rates in general go higher than what your bond pays, you may want to sell and buy a newer-issue bond which pays more. But with a market offering bonds yielding more than your original bond, who is going to buy it? You will probably have to sell at a small loss. The reverse is true if rates come down and your bond pays more than new issues. You could possibly sell your bond for more than you paid.

In the case of tax-free-bond mutual funds, a very nice option is available. In the event that interest rates increase and your share values decline, most funds have a reinvestment provision. This allows you to reinvest the income in order to buy more shares while the market is, hopefully, temporarily down—an example of dollar-cost averaging.

One disadvantage of tax-exempt bonds is that the interest rates they pay are usually lower than other bonds. However, considering the fact that the interest is tax free, the after-tax equivalent may be comparable. The higher tax bracket you are in, the better off you are.

## Limited Partnerships

As with any investment, there will always be a few horror stories told by friends and acquaintances about former investment failures in limited partnerships. However, most of these horror experiences can be avoided by following some very basic—and often repeated—advice.

First of all, never make a decision immediately. Do some checking into the reputation of the investment company; find out about its experience in the field and the track record of the general partner, the person whom you will give your money to and entrust to manage your funds. Your decision should also be directed by your personal financial status. Ask yourself how this investment will affect your savings reserve, cash flow, tax liability, and emotional comfort level.

The benefits of limited partnerships are many. Programs in million-dollar increments have the ability to put together investment deals that most individuals are not able to accomplish. Each partnership, regardless of the kind of investment involved, makes available to the individual investor all the benefits that he would normally receive had he attempted to do it himself. In owning a limited partnership, not only do you receive most of the tax benefits, but also you let someone else do all the work and take all the risk. The general partner provides the expertise, legal counsel, and accounting services in order to provide you with a yearly tax statement necessary to supplement your tax return. The general partner can protect you in most cases from the liability of lawsuits if something goes wrong. (This protection is important and should be confirmed as part of the package of any limited partnership you become involved in.) The general partner also provides the various contacts with other investors, giving you the opportunity to become a member of a large organization that can move with a great deal of force and power in the market place.

The question, "Should I invest in this type of program?", is brought up quite often, and I can only answer with a question. I ask the individual what his time is worth. Can he afford to take on the various tasks necessary to make such an investment on his own? The tasks may range from the creation of an investment idea to locating property or equipment; from traveling to inspect various properties or businesses to auditing books; from inspecting premises or equipment structures to settling employee disputes. Other major considerations in doing it yourself are the time and energy necessary to acquire the appropriate financing, prepare necessary legal documents, raise capital for the investments and/or establish credit at a bank, accept personal liability, and manage and maintain the investment.

There is no doubt that if the individual's venture is profitable, he will keep more profits and not have to share them with others. However, much more than money has been sacrificed. The investment or business may profit or fail due to the individual's experience and efficiency. I encourage people who would like to do it themselves to get involved in a pursuit they know extremely well, are good at, and will thoroughly enjoy.

### Real Estate Limited Partnerships

As discussed earlier, one of the most basic needs of the human being is shelter. Because of this need, real estate has almost always been in demand. Real estate and its structures are utilized nearly 24 hours a day—while we are having breakfast at home or lunch in the cafeteria, while we are working in the office during the day, or while we sleep at night in our homes.

As cities grow, the demand for local real estate increases, and prices rise. To second-guess and capitalize on the growth of a specific location demands knowledge, time, research, and money. Many people, therefore, choose to become involved in group investment programs which will provide many of the same benefits as buying directly but reduce various risks and liabilities.

The real estate limited partnership is managed usually by a co-owner, referred to as the general partner. The general partner creates a plan and an organization to purchase various properties, manage them, and ultimately sell them for a profit. The general partner invests some dollars, but mostly time and experience.

The limited partner—the co-owner—is required to invest cash into the program to provide the general partner with working capital. At this point, a partnership between the limited partners and the general partner begins. The investor has a share of ownership in a particular investment program, thus maintaining owner's equity growth and various tax benefits while reducing the liability of "doing it yourself." This type of partnership passes along most of the income, profits, and tax benefits to the limited partner. When tax benefits are available to the investor, this investment is referred to as a "tax shelter" limited partnership.

The limited partnership usually tends to have a life span of over five years before the investor gets all his money back. This is only reality. If you as an individual invested large sums into real estate, you would have to wait several years for the real estate to appreciate above and beyond the original attorney fees, real estate commissions, accounting fees, printing costs, appraisals, maintenance, and other expenses. In real estate, your future profits are actually made going into the deal or at the time of purchase. Some of the profits in a limited partnership go to the general partner to compensate for his time spent researching various properties and his years of management.

However, remember the various tax benefits passed on to you, the investor: fees and expenses charged to the partnership; interest expense on real estate loans; and depreciation allowances on properties. For example, in the case of the highly-leveraged programs—where the partnership buys several large buildings and projects at a cost appreciably more than the monies invested—the investor is allowed to use the full depreciation allowance on properties many times more valuable than his original investment.

Keep in mind that there is a cost for every tax benefit received. It may be in the amount of expense to the partnership or degree of risk assumed by the limited partners. However, on a positive note, the investor is usually protected from excessive personal expenses, aggravation and time involved in doing it himself. If the market does move up, the investor is in a good position to cash in on good timing, property management, and an upswing in the economy.

How are you to know if the general partner is practicing proper management of your money and the real estate it purchases? Well, in most programs, the general partner does not profit if you do not profit; he, too, has a vested interest in success. I would suggest dealing with partnerships that are registered with the Securities and Exchange Commission (SEC) on the national level or the Department of Corporations on the state level. This registration does not insure the partnership in any way. However, it will clarify if you are a limited partner or a general partner, an important distinction when dealing with legal liability, and it also outlines future responsibilities of the limited partner that might exist in the program.

## Oil and Gas Limited Partnerships

Like other natural resources, oil and gas are precious commodities that our country tends to treat with varying attitudes. When oil is plentiful, the nation's policies and tax legislation tend to ignore the importance of this country's becoming more self-sufficient and less dependent upon other nations for its uncontrollable addiction for energy supplies. This predicament can only be solved by good political relations with countries that supply oil and gas and a possible reduction of dependency upon them by producing our own oil and gas reserves.

There are various ways that the investor may become involved in the ownership of oil and gas businesses. The least desirable is being the consumer at the pump who receives no tax benefits for its consumption. We will be required to accept any increase in prices, regardless of the effect upon our personal finances. Another basic way to become involved is to simply purchase stock shares of oil companies that might be listed on the various stock exchanges. Here again we will receive little or no tax benefit. Our stock investment is at the hands of the public's emotional reactions to political and economic turmoil which fluctuate the value of our stock on a daily basis.

This leaves us with a very popular alternative to the dilemma of being a consumer without control: oil and gas limited partnerships. Be aware that there are not only various tax differences among these tax shelters but also many varieties of oil and gas programs themselves. Risk need not be a factor in this investment of widening opportunities.

*Oil and gas income funds* offer the limited partner the opportunity to own a small portion of an outfit which will pool all the investors' capital, then go out into the oil fields and purchase oil in the ground that someone else has already found. What you are doing here is buying oil at or below wholesale price and extracting it efficiently, then marketing it to various oil companies throughout the country. Your profits in this type of program are produced by the ability of the partnership to purchase the oil and gas reserves in the ground at an extremely low price because the partnership cashes out the people who did the actual drilling. "Cash is king," and we are about to make a profit from our invested cash. We have purchased our inventory at what we hope will be a very profitable price. Our income will be produced by the mark-up of our inventory of oil and gas, a mark-up which produces income in such a way that part of the income we receive is a return of our original investment. So far we have not experienced risk and thus receive little or no tax write-off other than a small depletion allowance which shelters some of our income from taxation because it is, quite simply, a return of our original investment capital.

There are many positive aspects to oil and gas income funds. You may or may not consider the income fund a tax shelter, but there are built-in tax breaks, such as receiving a depletion allowance on income. This means that when the fund pays dividends, not all of the amount is taxable. The basic economic potential for these funds is that you receive income from selling oil and gas after a mark-up in price, but the reserves in the ground might sell for considerably more than the fund paid if prices of oil and gas rise. This investment allows you to own a piece of the well and share in the profits when the country is once again at the mercy of oil prices.

One of the risks of oil and gas income funds is that the partnership might pay too much for the oil and gas reserves, pumping equipment, supplies, labor, and land leases. This excess, as well as major reduction in oil prices, could cause the program to lose value. Some partnerships—according to stories—have actually gone to the bank to borrow funds on future production hopes in order to pay out investors' distribution of income.

*Oil and gas drilling programs* have become popular tax shelters. The government wants more oil and gas to be found so they give tax breaks to anyone who tries to find some. Thus, an oil drilling program offers tax deductions *and* a potential for large profits if you strike oil. Unfortunately, drilling for oil is a very risky proposition. If you don't strike oil, you will lose money despite any tax savings.

It is very important that you examine the drilling program before you invest. Some programs may require you to put up more money later on so read the prospectus carefully. Look at the track record of the program. While past performance cannot be guaranteed in the future, it is better to invest in a program with a good track record than a bad one.

## Equipment Leasing Limited Partnerships

Equipment leasing is another way to reduce your taxes on portfolio income. In a leasing program, the money you contribute is used to buy equipment. This equipment may consist of railroad cars, trucks, trailers, airplanes, cars, shipping containers, computers, medical equipment, and even cable television systems. This equipment is then rented out. You are allowed to depreciate the equipment values, an allowance which shelters the income you receive from leasing the equipment. However, any money made on the resale over the depreciated cost of the equipment will be taxed at ordinary income rates. Leasing programs vary just as much as real estate programs.

If the program leverages—that is, borrows from the bank to buy more equipment than covered by dollars you have invested—you can receive a higher write-off. In return for the high write-off, the lease income received will go toward paying off the debt. The IRS will tax you on the lease income even though you never see a dime because it is going to pay the debt. Hopefully the depreciation allowance helps offset this negative.

Another issue to consider is the resale value of the equipment. The value depends on the type of equipment originally purchased in the fund. For high resale value, buying "low tech" equipment that will not become obsolete is best. For example, truck trailers will be useful long after you have wrung out all of their tax advantages. If your leasing program buys and leases computers, a new and better computer may have come on to the market, forcing your partnership to sell equipment at a very low price when it is time to sell.

In periods of high inflation, used equipment tends to have a high resale value. The value may even be equal to or greater than the original purchase price. In a period of low inflation and a stable or recessionary economy, the price received for the equipment will be much lower.

In concept, equipment leasing is the opposite of real estate programs. In the latter, you hope for appreciation of property over the long run. In equipment, tax benefits and high income are received up front. The bottom line of equipment leasing is that it provides tax breaks, tax-sheltered income, and some possible appreciation.

## Research and Development Limited Partnerships

America's successes are due to innovation. New products and ideas are the primary vehicles of prosperity and productivity. Historically, most new ideas and inventions originate with individuals. Many had to commit themselves to years of struggle. Others were able to line up wealthy investors to back their projects. The wealthy backers received tax breaks for their contributions as well as the potential to make a lot of money and the satisfaction involved in bringing an idea to fruition.

Limited partnerships are available to finance inventions or new products. Limited partnerships allow non-millionaires to participate in the adventure of creation.

Because of the lengthy process of creating, establishing, producing, and selling a new product, these types of programs usually tend to last longer than most other limited partnerships. They also carry some risk. The project you are investing in will not generate steady income or appreciate with a growing economy. Every step from conception to marketing must be properly executed in order to make a profit. If it hits, your profits may be tremendous.

Research and development must be considered within the context of your situation. While this should be true of all investments, it is especially true of research and development because of its long-term nature and risk. The main reason to invest in research and development is the potential for huge profits.

## Agriculture Limited Partnerships

Various agricultural partnerships are formed every year and can add a little diversity to your choice of investment opportunities. These partnerships might range from the producing of a new coffee bean to growing popular indoor plants. Like any other limited partnership, these programs are only as good as the management of the general partner, the product produced, and the market where it will be sold.

Keeping to the basics of any investment, you should consider economic benefits over all other attractions to the program. This type of investment is easily misrepresented and misunderstood because few investors understand the true mechanics of the farming industry and its economy. Unlike real estate where many of us can relate to experiences in financing, agricultural communities are difficult to understand if you are not from the farming community, and therefore the programs require more research on your part about what the program will actually do; research often overlooked by the potential investor who is dazzled by a well-informed, well-prepared broker putting on an investment seminar. Because of the unpredictability of weather conditions and resale market prices, this kind of investment can be very risky.

## Cattle Breeding Limited Partnerships

Cattle breeding is a very risky venture because so many things can go wrong. Breeding requires expertise and luck on the part of the breeder. Disease, death, and poor beef prices may hound the program. Genetic engineering advances may make breeding obsolete before the particular program you purchase is finished. And the tax specifics of these programs are complex. Currently, you can take depreciation on your breeder cows but not on the newborns.

These programs can be difficult to understand and should be closely reviewed before investing.

## Tax-Shelter Debriefing

So far we have reviewed a few different types of tax-sheltered programs available to the general public. While many of these programs will differ in the specific from those mentioned here, the basic elements will usually remain the same. They are basically structured to give the investor the opportunity to receive various tax benefits and to shelter other portfolio income. They do not require huge capital or expertise. They usually pass on most or all of the tax benefits created by the partnership to the investor.

Because the different tax benefits available to us as limited partners seem wonderful, we must be careful not to purchase these types of investments strictly for tax benefits. Competent counseling in the area of tax planning is necessary to determine if a specific tax shelter investment is right for you in any given year.

It is strongly advisable that the investment have economic merit and that you fully understand all of the advantages and drawbacks relating to the investment. A mistake in this area could mean the loss of hundreds or thousands of dollars by simply choosing a tax shelter that may be right for someone else but is completely wrong for you.

The tax-sheltered limited partnership is one of the most advantageous investment vehicles for public investors today. However, they are most complicated instruments, and in order to properly benefit, you should be fully aware of all the facts.

The following steps might help you decide whether to invest or not:

1. Consider the basic economic benefits of the investment first. Is it sound?

2. Check the reputation of the general partner.

3. Compare the track record of the general partner and the partnership itself to others on the market.

4. Determine whether you can hold the investment for several years.

5. Ask your accountant to prepare a tax estimate which should reflect the tax effect of the partnership on your tax return.

6. Take into consideration the time your money will be tied up, the risks involved with the invesment itself, and the tax savings available. Add them up and decide if the tax shelter should be considered.

While any investment involves some risk, the tax shelter reduces that risk by adding back instant profits created by tax benefits. Reducing taxes is a major consideration, but your assets can grow as well. But first, you must consider all the strings attached. This research of the investment and economics is called "due diligence." Do it well, and you will prosper!

Hearst Castle, CA

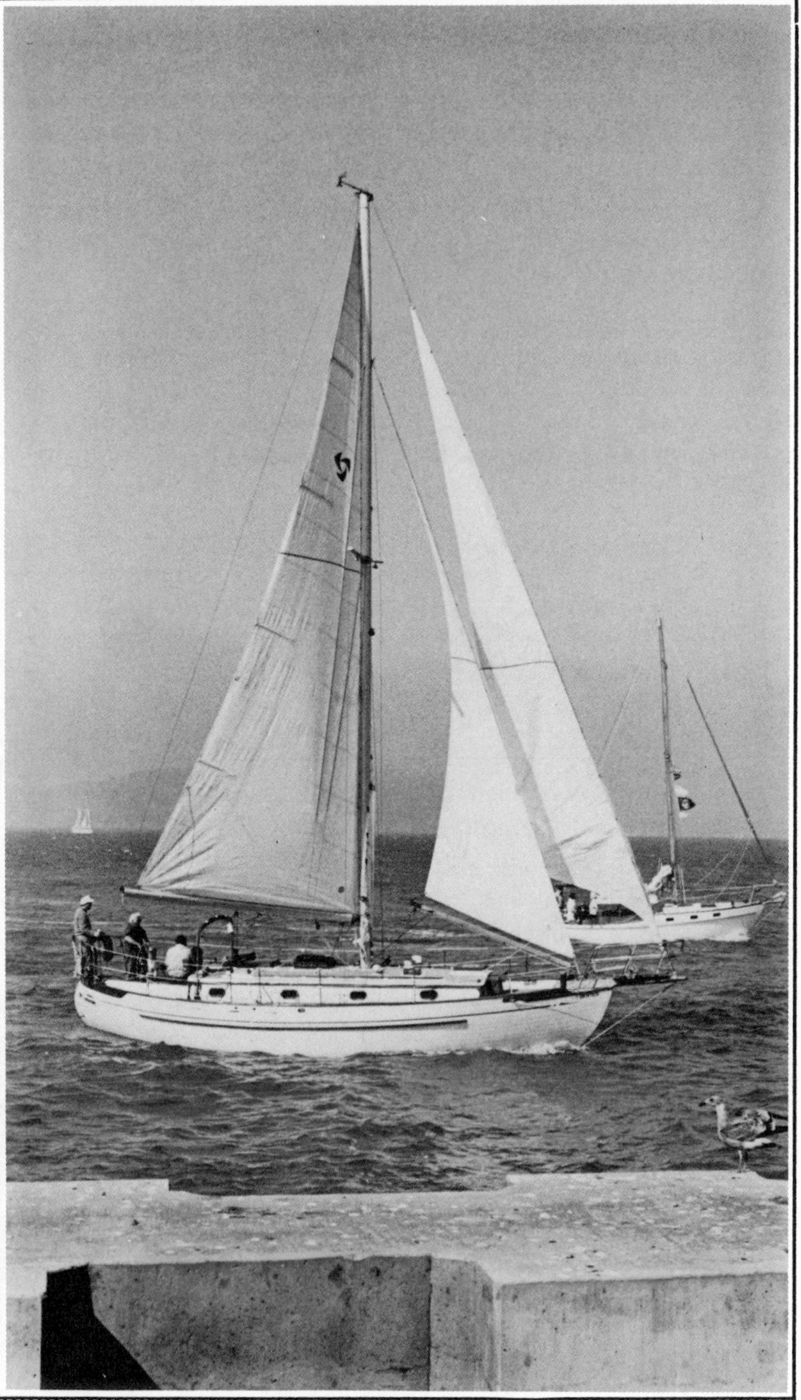

# THE SPECIFICS OF INSURANCE

Like most people, I really don't enjoy paying insurance premiums that come due each month or year. What a boring expense! You make no profits. You can only, at best, be paid back for your losses if you experience an unpleasant occurrence. However, in order to reduce your risk of losing all that you have worked and sacrificed for, in order to protect your assets as well as your estate, it is essential that you insure against possible catastrophes which could wipe out what you have and what you are trying to create. If there is ever a weak point in financial planning, it is in the area of preventing and/or insuring against risk which could totally destroy your estate over night. Therefore, it is important for you to know exactly what financial risk you are dealing with on a day-to-day basis.

It would be extremely difficult for you to make a living if you were unable to work or if you had been sued and lost your business due to misfortune or accident. What would happen to your family if you depended on two incomes to maintain a lifestyle and one income disappeared due to death?

There are an alarming number of court settlements in the six (and higher) figure range due to various unintentional accidents. If you own rental property, run a business, or have minor children, you are liable for other people's actions. Your tenants in a rental property might own a dog and not inform you. If the dog gets out of the backyard through a hole in the fence and bites someone, you might be named in a lawsuit for damages. God forbid the dog causes serious injury to a small child or takes a life! If you own a business with employees, you become responsible for their actions—not to mention full responsibility for any products sold or services rendered. As you know, you are financially and sometimes legally responsible for the actions of your children.

And so, fun though it may not be, you need to list all the disasters you can imagine that would cripple your financial future and then research the most economic ways to cover those disasters through insurance.

## Medical Insurance

Medical insurance is designed to cover expenses incurred as a result of an illness or accident. It is the most important type of insurance to have because if you are uninsured and become injured or ill, you could end up owing thousands upon thousands of dollars to doctors and hospitals.

There are two types of medical coverage plans:

1. *Health Maintenance Organization (HMO).* Here the individual belongs to a group, or HMO, program where he must go to a specific hospital. This is both good and bad. You may not know the doctor who sees you, but the expense of frequent visits or large bills is covered under an "umbrella." You don't have large deductibles or co-insurance provisions that require that you pay part of the total bill.

2. The other is co-insurance. In this plan, the insurance company pays 80–90% of the claim and the patient pays the remaining 10–20% until he has paid out a certain dollar amount previously specified.

It is extremely important that you know what illnesses, accidents, and benefits are *not* covered under your insurance. The most obvious example of omission is maternity benefits. Never take it for granted that maternity hospitalization and surgical coverage is provided. Often, maternity benefits are specifically excluded except for related complications at birth, and since hospitalization is expensive, having a baby can easily run into thousands of dollars. Also, certain experimental operations, which could save your life, might not be covered by many insurance companies.

*Don't wait until it is too late!* The best time to examine your coverage is not when you are in the hospital, but before you need the coverage. Ignorance will not be excused; you will be liable for uncovered expenses regardless. If you are not covered, you may be forced to liquidate your investments to pay bills. Please don't assume anything in the area of insurance. Be sure you are covered.

## Disability Insurance

Most people acquire an estate by working at a job over a long period of time. They work for income and save until they reach a point when their investments will work for them. Until that time, any loss of income due to a disability could cause a severe financial crisis for them and their families.

Disability should not be taken lightly. It is more of a financial hardship on the family if you become disabled than if you die. If you are adequately covered during your disability, that monthly check, however small, will reduce emotional anxieties felt by the family and you.

If you fail to plan your disability estate, you may be faced with a living death. If an injury that ultimately results in your disability occurs, you may be forced to draw on your retirement program, liquidate stocks, bonds, or savings just to survive. You need to look for sources of income that you can rely on if you or your spouse become disabled.

You must stop and ask yourself: "If I were disabled, could I pay my current bills? Could I continue on my investment plans? Although unable to work, could I assist in relieving emotional pain and suffering?"

There may be various types of *protection available through your employer;* however, few provide adequate benefits. For example, many workers will have only sick leave available to them. Others may be fortunate enough to have a salary continuation plan for up to six months.

There may be some *special insurance benefits provided by the state* in which you live. If you are completely disabled and the disability will last more than one year, you may be eligible to receive social security benefits. However, the disability benefits seldom provide adequate disability insurance.

In analyzing your disability protection, collect specific and complete information on whatever types of coverage you currently have. For example:

1. How long must you be disabled before your insurance will begin paying you benefits? This is called the elimination period.

2. What is the definition of disability according to your insurance company? Are you covered for an inability to perform your previous occupation only or to perform any occupation? For example, if you are a surgeon and lose the use of your hands, are you disabled because you can no longer practice surgery? Make sure your policy specifies. Some policies say that before you are covered you must be so bad off that you can't perform any occupation, including selling pencils on the street corner. Don't take it for granted that you are covered. Chances are you are not covered as well as you think you are.

3. What are the costs to you and/or your employer for the insurance?

4. How long will the disability income benefits continue? Many continue for one, three, five years, or some until age 65.

5. Will the disability income be taxed? Usually, disability income received is tax free.

Don't ignore this topic. As soon as you have one free moment, find out where you stand if you become disabled. Do not take someone else's word for it. Keep searching until you have documented proof of the amount of coverage you have. Usually for less than the price of a few meals out per month, you can protect your family from a worse financial tragedy than death. You also protect yourself from financial dependency on others for day-to-day existence.

## Life Insurance

Death is a reality. Furthermore, an untimely death is made more tragic if the bereaved must suffer financially as well. Yet life insurance is one of the most controversial types of insurance policies. Because of aggressive selling tactics, we have grown to dislike life insurance. Many people do not know if they really need insurance. If they do realize the need for it, they do not know how much or what kind. Some policies have proved costly to the insured. Outdated insurance that no longer meets our needs, and the bad reputation of life insurance companies have turned people off to the idea of life insurance even though they have a need for it. We refuse to purchase coverage for fear of "being sold."

Life insurance is nonetheless, and in most cases, necessary to a prosperous future. The type and quantity depend on your need in the overall picture of your financial plan. Keep in mind a few basic premises as you determine your individual needs.

1. Consider carefully when life insurance shopping because the insurance company is going to take care of itself first and worry about you second. Sales tactics using fear convince many of us to purchase the wrong type of coverage. You really cannot know what type of insurance or how much coverage you will need until you do an in-depth analysis of your total financial picture.

2. The cost of life insurance is based on the statistical probability of the insured's dying. The higher the chance of death's occuring, the more expensive the coverage.

3. Regardless of what a salesperson leads us to believe, most policies are going to end up costing the buyer something. Although many of

us definitely need temporary coverage over the next decade or so, life-long coverage can be substituted by continuous savings and investment programs.

4. Most retired people who have no dependents or whose spouses are provided for by retirement income, don't usually need life insurance. However, if they still have whole life policies, they may be able to liquidate for cash value and invest the money for income or even take a vacation. Drawing the funds out of the policy doesn't usually cause a tax problem because the excess cash usually represents previous overcharges of premiums. (I am not discounting the importance of life insurance; I am simply pointing out that more efficient methods are available for life insurance coverage and retirement accumulation.)

5. The amount of coverage you buy should correlate with the protection needed.

Simply put, you might consider three levels of protection and choose the most appropriate to your goals:

1. *Minimum coverage.* You buy a life insurance policy that would provide just enough cash at your death to pay off all the loans and debts that you have incurred. This does not necessarily include the full mortgage but possibly enough cash to provide an income equal to yours for one year.

2. *Medium coverage.* It is possible that you feel more cash would be needed to pay off all bills, including the mortgage, as well as provide enough income for the family to take its time re-adjusting, (say, enough cash to replace your income for three to five years). This is important if you have a non-working spouse who would need time to train for a profession, or if the children's educational expenses are planned.

3. *Maximum coverage.* This level of protection is designed to provide enough cash to replace a lifetime of income and enough cash to replace the future estate you never had the chance to provide. In this case you could easily be talking about $500,000 to $1,000,000 worth of coverage.

What do you do now in your planning? Much the same as you have been doing. Research. Locate and study all the life insurance policies you currently have. You may be covered through an employer's group insurance plan, through your credit union, your bank card, your car insurance. Understanding what coverages you have can help you avoid buying too much, or it can help you fill the gaps where you are undercovered. You will need the actual policies to find out exactly what coverages you have and the terms of benefit collection. You will also need to review your policies with someone other than an insurance salesperson.

Before taking any measures to add, reduce, or discontinue your life insurance, let your financial planner or other advisors review your situation and your need for insurance within the context of your overall financial situation. You should never drop a policy and discontinue coverage until you are certain that another company has accepted you and will pay the policy amount without exception, or you are sure coverage is no longer needed.

## Homeowners' Insurance

The home is the single largest investment made by most people. They work years to save enough money for a down payment, and the monthly payments become the cornerstone of expenses. For most, buying and keeping a home is a struggle.

Whether you are still making payments, or you own your home free and clear, you are constantly in danger of losing it. Fires and natural disasters can destroy physical structures. Guests, passersby, mailmen—and even burglars—can sue you if they injure themselves on your property. Swimming pools—an "attractive nuisance" according to the courts—represent a major liability. People can slip and fall on the wet concrete around the pool. Even worse, someone can drown. Pool owners are required by law to take active measures to prevent neighborhood children from getting to the pool unsupervised.

Homeowners' insurance will protect you from these disasters. You need proper coverage in sufficient amount, and like any other type of insurance, your homeowners' should be coordinated in an overall plan to make sure all risks are covered and all limits are met.

The amount of coverage for fire and natural disasters is dependent on the present or replacement cost of rebuilding your home as well as replacing all the contents. I have observed alarmingly insufficient coverage in clients' homeowners' policies. For example, I once analyzed a policy that provided $41,000 for the rebuilding of a person's home. Due to inflation, the cost of rebuilding the home had escalated to $80,000. As you can see, the homeowner would have been nearly $40,000 short.

In the area of liability, most policies will provide coverage in case someone is injured on your property. This coverage, called medical coverage, usually covers the injured for a few thousand dollars without argument and is designed to prevent the injured party's suing for medical bills and damages. However, if an injury is serious or permanent, you can count on a much larger settlement, many times resulting in lengthy court battles. If your liability coverage is not enough to cover the settlement amount, you can be found liable and can lose assets as well as future income. This is why you must keep in touch with your insurance agent and inform him/her of your current insurance needs. It may be boring to review the coverage, but the occasional review may very well save your financial life.

## Automobile Insurance

Cars are a useful and even a vital tool in this fast-paced society, yet they are a lethal weapon. Each year approximately 50,000 people die as a result of auto accidents, and millions are injured. Each year, billions of dollars are lost in wages, property damage, and legal and medical costs due to automobile accidents. Therefore, automobile insurance is not only advisable but necessary in order to cover yourself against damage to your car and injury to yourself and others. You could be sued for hundreds of thousands, even millions of dollars to support a victim of an accident for the rest of his or her life. Many states will revoke or suspend yor driver's license if you do not have auto insurance.

It is vital that individuals and businesses maintain, inspect, and update their current coverages. Inflation may have eaten away at your maximum coverage. Court settlements increase each year. Do not get caught short. Make sure you carry enough insurance.

Auto insurance is basically broken down into the following framework:

*Liability* coverage is the most important. Your policy will indicate your coverage as 100/300 (or whatever amount you have chosen). These figures translate that you have a maximum coverage of $100,000 for each person involved in an accident. However, if four people are injured and you are sued, the policy limits the total to $300,000. Each of the four might receive a lesser amount, but if the damages awarded by the judge are $100,000 per person, the missing $100,000 will come out of your present estate. If you don't have it, the court can attach future earnings.

*Uninsured motorist* is—or should be—built into your policy. You and your passengers are insured against the other driver if he is at fault but has no insurance. If he has coverage, but is not covered for the full amount needed, your policy, if it has this provision, will also cover you. Make sure both these coverages are high enough.

*Medical coverage* pays out immediately for medical expenses in order to prevent litigation.

*Property damage* is also an important section in the policy. If you damage someone's property, repair costs could be tens of thousands of dollars.

In order to intelligently determine your coverage, make sure that you inform your auto insurance agent of your estate values and desires of full and high coverages. It would be better to lose a few dollars a year to overcoverage than to experience a freak accident that leaves you bankrupt after litigation. I figure it this way, if the worst should ever happen and someone was seriously injured, I would want that person compensated in every way possible. If I were undercovered and forced into a bankruptcy because I couldn't pay the victim of an accident his due compensation, we would both lose. I would now carry not only the guilt of having unintentionally hurt someone, but also the knowledge that I had failed to financially make it up to that person. Don't let these coverages go uninspected. Protecting what you have is more important than any investment program. It may take a lifetime to acquire an estate and just a brief moment to lose it.

## Liability Protection

General liability is probably the most important coverage you can have. The courts are ripe with multimillion dollar lawsuits, and in order to protect your assets from the needy or greedy hands of others, you need liability insurance. No one plans to be sued; yet the danger exists. Your hard-earned assets could be taken away from you in a court judgment. The more you own the more you have to lose.

Many times liability insurance is a part of home and auto insurance, but many people will need additional liability coverage.

*Business liability.* Increasingly, the courts are giving tenants of rental property more and more rights at the expense of the property owners. Landlords can be sued for any number of reasons. For example, a water pipe could burst or electrical wiring could burn and cause damage to a tenant's property. While making repairs, a tenant could step on a nail. A tenant may sue after slipping in the bath tub! A tenant can sue for invasion of privacy or wrongful eviction.

Self-employed people need liability insurance also. There is always the possibility that a customer will become injured or his property damaged resulting in a multimillion dollar lawsuit.

*Malpractice liability.* Have you heard of malpractice insurance? Doctors are not the only professionals needing this insurance. Dentists and pharmacists need it too. Lawyers, architects, insurance agents, and financial planners should all have professional liability insurance. Many professionals can buy errors and omission insurance policies just in case they forget something in performing their service (which is bound to happen during a career). If "malpractice" occurs, the insurance policy will cover the problem.

*Personal liability policies* cover you and your family for personal risks. For example, you will be covered if someone sues you for injury or property damage. The policy usually covers you for injury occurring in your home, including those resulting from sports activities or damages that your pet may cause. Every time someone steps on your property, you could be liable for an injury lawsuit. It is now law in some states that if a person drives from your house under the influence of alcohol and has an accident, you can be held responsible.

## "Umbrella" Policies

The umbrella liability coverage basically picks up where your homeowners' or auto liability stops. Say your auto insurance offers $100,000 coverage to any person who wins a settlement against you, but a person is awarded more than the $100,000; an umbrella policy of $100,000 deductible will cover the additional. This type of policy is very inexpensive and a wonderful thing to have in time of need. However, make sure you know what perils or occurrences it will not cover. The worst mistake you can ever make, and we all do it, is to assume you are covered. If you match up the right policies and coverages, you can free yourself from the threat of paying a court settlement out of your own pocket.

## Insurance Debriefing

Throughout this section on insurance coverage, we have stressed the importance of protecting your assets. The world is a dangerous place, full of perils. It takes only a split second to have an auto accident, to lose your home by a spark igniting leaking gas, or to become disabled or die. A split second could ruin you and your family financially for the remainder of your lives.

This is why it is vital for you to have insurance of the proper types and amounts. Know what coverages you have. Read any existing policies, whether general liability or umbrella, automobile or medical, life or disability. If you don't have the policies, have your insurance agent prepare a list of coverages. If you don't have coverage, get some!

Once you have insurance, you must update and review it periodically. Although this task may be tedious, it may save you hundreds of thousands of dollars. Your insurance needs change, and if you do not update your policies, you may leave yourself exposed to additional risks or you may be paying premiums for a coverage you no longer need. Eliminating excess premiums is one thing, extending coverage is another. Make sure you are doing the right things.

Every person has different liabilities for different periods of time and different needs in amounts of coverage. Don't make the mistake of just listening to a friend about your needs. Find a good insurance agent or financial planner and be willing to pay the premiums for the coverage you need. Remember, you are going to be worth at least one million dollars some day. Let's make sure you can hang on to it.

# APPENDIX A
# THE WORKSHEETS

Mindy Richmon

# Monthly Budget
## of Family Expenses

**Liabilities**

Mortgage payment or rent      $_____

Real estate taxes      _____

Automobile loan      _____

Personal loan      _____

Credit card accounts      _____

Other      _____

Other      _____

    Total Liabilities      $_____

**Transportation**

Gas and oil      _____

Maintenance and repair      _____

Auto registration      _____

Public transportation      _____

Parking      _____

    Total Transportation      _____

**Insurance**

Life insurance      _____

Health insurance      _____

Disability insurance      _____

Auto insurance      _____

Homeowners' or renters' insurance      _____

Liability insurance      _____

    Total Insurance      _____

**Savings and Investment Contributions**

Savings accounts      _____

Certificates of deposit      _____

Stocks      _____

Bonds      _____

Other      _____

Other      _____

    Total Savings and Investments      _____

**Contributions**

Political      _____

Religious      _____

Charitable      _____

Other      _____

    Total Contributions      _____

## Household Expenses
Food and miscellaneous          _____
Gas and electricity             _____
Garbage                         _____
Telephone                       _____
Water                           _____
Maintenance and repair          _____
Children's allowances           _____
Gifts                           _____
Miscellaneous                   _____
Other                           _____
    Total Household Expenses          _____

## Personal Expenses
Clothing                        _____
Medical                         _____
Dental                          _____
Prescription drugs              _____
Recreation                      _____
Hobbies                         _____
Vacations                       _____
Books and magazines             _____
Other                           _____
    Total Personal Expenses          _____

    Total Monthly Expenses          $_____

Some expenses are not necessarily monthly expenses and should be divided accordingly. For example, an annual expense like auto registration should be divided by twelve.

# Balance Sheet or Net Worth Statement

## ASSETS

| | |
|---|---|
| Cash — checking | $_____ |
| — savings | _____ |
| Money market funds | _____ |
| Credit cards | _____ |
| Stocks | _____ |
| Mutual funds | _____ |
| Bonds | _____ |
| Real estate partnerships | _____ |
| Energy | _____ |
| R & D programs | _____ |
| Leasing partnerships | _____ |
| Other (L/P) | _____ |
| REITs | _____ |
| Retirement — annuity | _____ |
| — IRA | _____ |
| Real estate — rentals | _____ |
| — land | _____ |
| Tangibles | _____ |
| Notes | _____ |
| Other | _____ |
| **SUBTOTAL** | $_____ |

NET WORTH (exclusive of home, furnishings, autos) $_____

| | |
|---|---|
| Home | $_____ |
| Furnishings | _____ |
| Personal property | _____ |
| Autos | _____ |
| **SUBTOTAL** | $_____ |
| **TOTAL ASSETS** | $_____ |
| Less Liabilities | _____ |
| **TOTAL NET WORTH** | $_____ |

## LIABILITIES

| | |
|---|---|
| Credit cards | $_____ |
| Credit union loans | |
| Bank loans | _____ |
| Personal loans | _____ |
| Secured loans | _____ |
| Real estate loans | _____ |
| Other debts | _____ |
| Other | _____ |
| Other | _____ |
| | $_____ |
| Home mortgages | $_____ |
| Auto loans | _____ |
| | $_____ |
| **TOTAL LIABILITIES** | $_____ |

# APPENDIX B
# INVESTMENT CHARACTERISTICS AT A GLANCE

In this appendix we have created brief, at-a-glance, fact sheets for obtaining bottom line concepts about investment vehicles. The investments listed are not all the opportunities available; however, they are a majority, and familiarity with the analytical process will assist you in looking at other opportunities as well.

Each fact sheet will identify:

**TYPE OF INVESTMENT** and then present a breakdown by:

**DESCRIPTION** — Here we will briefly and basically describe a particular investment. Remember that this description is speaking in general terms and there may be various differences in investments of this type. This section is only meant to give you some idea of the investment topic.

**FEATURES AND BENEFITS** — Each feature will be given a score:

a minus (−) for lack of or low degree;
a zero    (0) indicating a neutral position; and
a plus    (+) showing a higher amount or more favorable degree.

These scores relate to the investment for the following features:

**Degree of Safety** — Here we are giving some idea of the basic degree of safety available through the investment; however, now investment is completely safe.

**Potential for Appreciation** — We will indicate whether it is felt that this investment has potential to increase in value in the future.

**Tax Benefits** — Various tax benefits may be available; we will indicate just a few. Keep in mind, as you read, that Congress is always busily at work changing tax laws.

**Liquidity** — Here we are concerned with the ease of converting an investment to cash.

**QUESTIONS FOR THE BROKER/INSTITUTION** —

We would like to point out various questions for a particular investment that you need answered. Whether you are ready to invest or you are attending investment classes, these questions will help you gain a better understanding and hopefully expose certain facts that may not be apparent.

(+) indicates favorable        (0) neutral        (−) undesirable

## TYPE: ANNUITIES

**DESCRIPTION** — An annuity is a contract between the investor and an insurance company. This contract is usually backed by the assets of the company and offers a guarantee to the investor that he will receive at least a minimum interest return on his money and a full return of his money at the completion of the term of the agreement. The annuity is basically a savings account that offers an additional benefit and is established with a life insurance company. Most often, as the interest accrues in these accounts, they are held as a retirement fund. The investor is allowed to accrue interest and not pay taxes on those earnings until retirement or the time money is withdrawn. These programs can offer interest on savings or put you into bonds and even stocks, thus offering more flexibility in your investment choices (but no guarantee of results).

**FEATURES AND BENEFITS** —

(+)    *Degree of Safety* — Monies are backed by the assets of the insurance company which are usually quite substantial. This is not true if you choose the bond or stock portfolio. The fixed savings account is the only guaranteed investment.

(−)    *Potential for Appreciation* — The annuity will earn income. However, the original amount invested will not unless you add the interest back to it. Growth may be available if stocks are utilized within the investment.

(+)    *Tax Benefits* — The interest earned is usually tax sheltered, but the original investment usually receives no tax benefits unless placed into a retirement program, such as a TSA. Some employees of non-profit organizations and schools can deduct the amount contributed as a supplement to their other retirement programs.

(+)    *Liquidity* — You can usually liquidate quite easily, but be extremely aware of various penalties and charges levied by the insurance company and IRS for doing so.

**QUESTIONS FOR THE BROKER/INSTITUTION** —

1.    What is the rating of the insurance company offering the annuity, and how safe is the company compared to others?

2.    What are the costs and penalties going into and coming out of the investment?

3.    What is the interest rate offered, and how and when will it fluctuate?

4.    What type of investments are held in this program? Is it a savings account, or are there stocks and bonds?

(+) indicates favorable          (0) neutral          (−) undesirable

## TYPE: BANK AND SAVINGS AND LOAN ACCOUNTS — SAVINGS

**DESCRIPTION** — Places to leave money for short periods of time. The money remains extremely accessible. You can walk into the bank and demand immediate cash from your account. This liquidity is not available in other kinds of accounts.

**FEATURES AND BENEFITS** —

(+)     *Degree of Safety* — Many banks are insured for accounts up to $100,000. Look for the bank's membership in or coverage by the Federal Depository Insurance Corporation (FDIC).

(−)     *Potential for Appreciation* — If inflation occurs, the balance stays the same; the only increase is interest earned.

(−)     *Tax Benefits* — No tax benefits exist for a standard account.

(+)     *Liquidity* — Can be liquidated immediately during banking hours.

**QUESTIONS FOR THE BROKER/INSTITUTION** —

1.     What interest will I earn and for how long? Does it compound daily, monthly, or quarterly?

2.     Are there penalties or loss of earning if I withdraw my funds?

3.     How often does the interest rate change?

4.     Is this account insured and if so by whom?

(+) indicates favorable          (0) neutral          (−) undesirable

# INVESTMENT CHARACTERISTICS AT A GLANCE

## TYPE: BANK AND SAVINGS AND LOAN ACCOUNTS — CERTIFICATES OF DEPOSIT

**DESCRIPTION** — CDs are issued by banks and various savings and loans. They vary in dollar amounts, interest rates, and time lengths. Maturity may range from weeks to years. This is a loan from the buyer of the CD to the bank or savings and loan institution for a specified period of time in return for interest paid to the buyer.

## FEATURES AND BENEFITS —

(+)     *Degree of Safety* — These investments are backed by the assets of the bank or savings and loan. Most institutions have federal insurance for depositors.

(−)     *Potential for Appreciation* — Only the amount of interest agreed upon and the principal are available to the purchaser.

(−)     *Tax Benefits* — Interest is fully taxable.

(0)     *Liquidity* — You must wait until maturity to liquidate without penalty. Provisions for liquidation do exist in some cases.

## QUESTIONS FOR THE BROKER/INSTITUTION —

1.      Is the institution insured by the federal government?

2.      What is the maturity of the CD?

3.      What are the liquidation costs?

4.      What happens to the interest as it is earned? Is it reinvested or paid in cash?

5.      Will the CD be renewed automatically without my instructions?

6.      What is the interest rate? Does it compound daily, monthly, or quarterly?

(+) indicates favorable          (0) neutral          (−) undesirable

## TYPE: BONDS

**DESCRIPTION** — An instrument that many large corporate or public institutions use to raise money. They sell bonds or a "promise to pay back principal with interest." The promise is usually backed by property or other assets that the bond holder or "creditor" can liquidate in emergencies. Bonds are usually rated for strength or dependability of the organization issuing the bonds. Bonds are simply lending agreements. The purchaser of the bond is the lender; the issuer is the borrower. If you purchase a bond, you become the lender.

## FEATURES AND BENEFITS —

(+)  *Degree of Safety* — Favorable if backed by substantial assets; however, market values can change if sold before maturity.

(−)  *Potential for Appreciation* — The borrower is only obligated to pay back the principle amount of the bond plus interest.

(0)  *Tax Benefits* — Most bond interest is taxable; but some, such as tax-free municipal bonds, provide tax-free interest at slightly lower interest rates.

(0)  *Liquidity* — Individual bonds do not liquidate until they mature, but they can be sold on the open market for cash. Bond funds or bond municipal funds usually provide liquidity.

## QUESTIONS FOR THE BROKER/INSTITUTION —

1.  When does this bond mature?

2.  What assets back this bond? Who is issuing this bond?

3.  How are the dividends taxed, and when are they paid?

4.  What is the rating of the bond?

(+) indicates favorable          (0) neutral          (−) undesirable

## TYPE: BONDS — CORPORATE

**DESCRIPTION** — These bonds are issued by larger corporations to raise capital for corporate expansion. These bonds (whch are actually loans made by the buyer) are backed by the corporation's assets. If the corporation has major financial difficulties and can't pay back bond holders, the bond holders are among the first to attach the assets for repayment of the bonds.

## FEATURES AND BENEFITS —

(0)  *Degree of Safety* — If the corporation issuing the bond is rated highly, its assets back the bond.

(−)  *Potential for Appreciation* — This is only a loan to the issuing corporation. Interest is the only profit, with some trading profits if practiced.

(−)  *Tax Benefits* — All interest is taxable with few tax benefits.

(+)  *Liquidity* — Most bonds can be sold prior to maturity; however, current bond values can change.

## QUESTIONS FOR THE BROKER/INSTITUTION —

1.  What is the rating of this bond?

2.  When does it mature?

3.  Can it be called prior to maturity? Will my money be paid back to me before the regular maturity date?

4.  How stable is the industry in which this corporate bond is held?

(+) indicates favorable        (0) neutral        (−) undesirable

## TYPE: BONDS — MUNICIPAL

**DESCRIPTION** — These bonds are issued by local governmental municipalities, states, hospitals, and other public facilities. The issuer's purpose is to raise monies needed for community projects at low interest rates. Because the government allows the bond buyer to receive interest free of tax, the lower rate of interest paid on the loan (bond) is attractive. If you buy the municipal bond in the state in which you live, the interest may be state-tax exempt as well as federal.

## FEATURES AND BENEFITS —

(+) *Degree of Safety* — There is some degree of risk; however, if you purchase high-rated bonds and hold them until maturity, you will be all right.

(−) *Potential for Appreciation* — You will only receive interest on the bond. The bond is a loan, not meant to appreciate.

(+) *Tax Benefits* — The interest is usually federal, and sometimes state, tax exempt.

(+) *Liquidity* — Most bonds can be readily sold on the open bond market.

## QUESTIONS FOR THE BROKER/INSTITUTION —

1. Who issues this bond?
2. What is its rating?
3. To what extent is it tax exempted?
4. When does it mature? Where can I sell?

(+) indicates favorable          (0) neutral          (−) undesirable

## TYPE: BONDS — UNIT TRUSTS

**DESCRIPTION** — Unit trusts are similar to mutual funds. They hold fixed portfolios of bonds; they have a pre-determined life span; and they produce income. As the bonds mature, the principle amounts are returned to the investor. The diversified portfolio of individual bonds offers more safety.

## FEATURES AND BENEFITS —

(+) *Degree of Safety* — Compared to individual bonds, the unit trust offers safety in numbers.

(−) *Potential for Appreciation* — Bonds historically have not been known to appreciate.

(0) *Tax Benefits* — Corporate bond unit-trust income is taxable. However, municipal bond unit trusts earn tax-free income.

(+) *Liquidity* — They can be traded on the open market.

## QUESTIONS FOR THE BROKER/INSTITUTION —

1. What is the rating of the bonds in the trust?

2. What is the tax status?

3. Can the securities (bonds) in the fund be called back by the issuer, and if so, when?

4. How can I liquidate if needed?

5. What fees are involved?

(+) indicates favorable      (0) neutral      (−) undesirable

## TYPE: BONDS — U.S. GOVERNMENT

**DESCRIPTION** — Interest-bearing loans made by the buyer to the U.S. Government for many national projects. These bonds vary in characteristics: different investment sizes, maturities. The interest is fully taxable at the federal level. The bonds are usually insured or backed by the government.

## FEATURES AND BENEFITS —

(+) *Degree of Safety* — Backed by the U.S. Government.

(−) *Potential for Appreciation* — Earn interest only.

(−) *Tax Benefits* — Taxable at the federal level.

(0) *Liquidity* — Liquid only at maturity; however, they can be sold on the bond market at current value.

## QUESTIONS FOR THE BROKER/INSTITUTION —

1. What specific type of bond is this?

2. What government agency backs it?

3. How do I liquidate if desired?

4. What are the fees or commissions?

(+) indicates favorable         (0) neutral         (−) undesirable

## TYPE: BONDS — ZERO COUPON

**DESCRIPTION** — These bonds are usually purchased from a brokerage house that has purchased a block of corporate or U.S. Government securities. These bonds mature at full value, and the value at maturity is based on an assumed yield or interest rate. If interest rates drop, the investor can sell the bond at a profit because his bond earns more than the going rates. If interest rates rise, the resale value can decline.

## FEATURES AND BENEFITS —

(+)  *Degree of Safety* — If held to maturity, principal will be returned. If sold prematurely, market value can fluctuate.

(−)  *Potential for Appreciation* — Bonds are not structured for appreciation. If interest rates drop below the bond's yield, the value can rise. However, appreciation is not expected.

(−)  *Tax Benefits* — The interest earned, although not paid to you until maturity, is taxable each year. Zero coupon bonds that are structured with municipal bonds, however, accrue interest free of tax.

(0)  *Liquidity* — The bonds themselves must mature before liquidating; however, they can be sold on the open market.

## QUESTIONS FOR THE BROKER/INSTITUTION —

1.  How long until the bond(s) mature?

2.  What yield to maturity will be earned?

3.  Am I taxed on income I am not receiving each year?

4.  How do I sell the bond, and what is the cost to do so?

(+) indicates favorable          (0) neutral          (−) undesirable

## TYPE: CASH

**DESCRIPTION** — Legal tender or currency used for financial transactions. If not invested, it will not provide income of any kind. The international value or purchasing power of the dollar can change.

## FEATURES AND BENEFITS —

(+) *Degree of Safety* — The American dollar is backed by the government; however, its purchasing power is always at risk.

(−) *Potential for Appreciation* — With the exception of increased purchasing power internationally, here at home it does not increase in value.

(−) *Tax Benefits* — Offers no tax benefit except for donations to charity.

(+) *Liquidity* — Cash is the ultimate source of liquidity for trading.

## QUESTIONS FOR THE BROKER/INSTITUTION —

1.   Not applicable.

(+) indicates favorable          (0) neutral          (−) undesirable

## TYPE: COLLECTIBLES

**DESCRIPTION** — Any item that has the potential to increase in value or resell for more than the original purchase price. These types of items can range from china plates, dolls, paintings, and furniture to automobiles, tractors, and tools. Virtually anything that increases its value with age falls into this category.

### FEATURES AND BENEFITS —

(−)  *Degree of Safety* — Safety is determined by demand. Many of these items are difficult to store. Loss due to theft is a concern.

(+)  *Potential for Appreciation* — Many items can continue to appreciate, providing they remain popular and in demand.

(0)  *Tax Benefits* — Profits at sale are fully taxed; however, they accumulated with no tax liability.

(−)  *Liquidity* — You must find a buyer, and demand can fluctuate. There are auctions, but auction fees can be very high.

### QUESTIONS FOR THE BROKER/INSTITUTION —

1.    How can I be sure this item is an original?

2.    Are there auctions available for reselling the item?

3.    Are there publications regarding this item?

4.    Where can I store this item, and what does it cost to insure it?

(+) indicates favorable          (0) neutral          (−) undesirable

4444

## TYPE: COLLECTIBLES — ART

**DESCRIPTION** — Art can vary from the more sophisticated painting to an unknown sculpture you made in your college art class. The value of art is, of course, difficult to determine and is usually in the eye of the beholder. However, some pieces can be so highly valued that the true value is unknown by the average individual.

## FEATURES AND BENEFITS —

(−) *Degree of Safety* — This type of investment is vulnerable to theft and fluctuations in public interest.

(+) *Potential for Appreciation* — Art has historically done very well over the years and kept pace with inflation.

(−) *Tax Benefits* — For the average person, there are no tax breaks for investing in art.

(−) *Liquidity* — While art is readily transferable, it may be hard to find a buyer despite the frequent art auctions in New York.

## QUESTIONS FOR THE BROKER/INSTITUTION —

1. Obtain an authority's estimate of value, and ask your broker to provide proof.

2. Who grades the value of this type of investment?

3. Where can I compare this piece of art and confirm its value?

4. If I desire to liquidate, what type of market is available?

(+) indicates favorable     (0) neutral     (−) undesirable

## TYPE: "FEATURES" — COMMODITIES — CONTRACTS

**DESCRIPTION** — Two parties sign a contract wherein one party agrees to deliver a specified product or commodity at a pre-determined price. Both parties are at risk if the present price of the item changes. For example, with wheat as the commodity, the farmer and customer agree on a price for the wheat sale months into the future. If the price of wheat rises, the customer has a contract stating he can buy it at the old price and can now turn around and sell it on the market for a profit; the farmer loses out on being able to sell it at the newer price. If the price declines, however, the customer is on the hook for the full, agreed-upon contract price.

## FEATURES AND BENEFITS —

(−)  *Degree of Safety* — Futures are extremely volatile because prices of the commodity can fluctuate widely.

(+)  *Potential for Appreciation* — If your speculation on price changes in your favor, major profits may occur.

(−)  *Tax Benefits* — No beneficial tax treatment exists.

(0)  *Liquidity* — Contracts can be traded on the open market or you can wait until expiration, but values can fluctuate.

## QUESTIONS FOR THE BROKER/INSTITUTION —

1.  What commodity does this contract represent?

2.  Is this contract leveraged? Exactly how much can I lose?

3.  Where is this futures contract traded?

4.  What are my costs and commissions in buying and selling?

(+) indicates favorable          (0) neutral          (−) undesirable

## TYPE: LIFE INSURANCE

**DESCRIPTION** — A contract with the life insurance company agreeing that if the insured dies, the designated beneficiary receives a pre-agreed cash settlement. This cash settlement and other additional savings plans in the policy qualify life insurance as an investment. Because of strong lobbying, life insurance companies create policies that have the ability to accumulate cash reserves, make non-taxable distribution from tax-sheltered savings funds as loans to its owner, and other interesting concepts. However, these concepts are many times extremely confusing and require much thought. This is a product that can offer many valuable features.

## FEATURES AND BENEFITS —

(+) *Degree of Safety* — Most are backed by very conservative assets of the company.

(−) *Potential for Appreciation* — Most savings accounts within the policy, called cash reserves, have little potential for keeping pace with inflation. However some are structured for growth.

(+) *Tax Benefits* — Cash reserves and other funds can accumulate tax shelters.

(+) *Liquidity* — Most life insurance policies can be easily liquidated.

## QUESTIONS FOR THE BROKER/INSTITUTION —

1. What kind of policy is this, i.e., whole life, universal life, term?

2. What is the actual life insurance premium or cost of the insurance?

3. How much of my premium goes to my savings or investment plan?

4. Are there penalties to withdraw, and what are the upfront costs and commissions?

(+) indicates favorable          (0) neutral          (−) undesirable

## TYPE: LIMITED PARTNERSHIPS — LEASING PROGRAMS

**DESCRIPTION** — Most leasing programs available to the public come in the form of a leasing limited partnership. Here you purchase units of a group project that is put together to purchase various kinds of business equipment. This equipment is then leased to companies for income. Here all tax benefits are passed along to the investment partners along with some or all of the lease income. If the partnership buys the equipment in the program for cash, the income from the leases will all go to you, the investor. However, if the fund borrows to buy more equipment than monies raised, parts of the lease income on the equipment will go to paying off its loans.

## FEATURES AND BENEFITS —

(0)  *Degree of Safety* — The type of equipment purchased and the leverage of financing determine the program's safety.

(−)  *Potential for Appreciation* — Some appreciation to equipment could happen if inflation occurs; however, depreciation in equipment values is inevitable.

(+)  *Tax Benefits* — Substantial tax deductions are available against income.

(−)  *Liquidity* — The units don't have a ready market. Units can be sold, but the selling is difficult. Many programs run from seven to 15 years in length.

## QUESTIONS FOR THE BROKER/INSTITUTION —

1.  What type of equipment is to be purchased in the program?
2.  Will there be leveraging or borrowing to buy more equipment?
3.  Will I receive all applicable tax benefits?

(+) indicates favorable            (0) neutral            (−) undesirable

## TYPE: LIMITED PARTNERSHIPS — PRIVATE PLACEMENTS

**DESCRIPTION** — Privates are structured for the more sophisticated investors. Private placement or small partnership investment, in many instances, is exempt from securities regulations. In addition, this type of investment offers a quicker turnaround time because of less red tape, tends to be much more aggressive than public limited partnerships, and is small in size with fewer investors than public programs. Since there is less regulation for these programs, the investor is usually left on his own, and the investor needs to be well informed before investing.

## FEATURES AND BENEFITS —

(0) *Degree of Safety* — It depends on what the partnership is investing in and how the program is structured.

(+) *Potential for Appreciation* — Potential for a greater return assumes higher risk.

(+) *Tax Benefits* — Since many privates use a high degree of borrowing in the fund, tax benefits are substantially enhanced.

(−) *Liquidity* — Generally, there is no market for privates. In fact, many privates require additional future investments.

## QUESTIONS FOR THE BROKER/INSTITUTION —

1. Does the program require additional investments and does it have stage pay in requirements?

2. How much leveraging or borrowing will be done to purchase the property in the program?

3. Who is the general partner(s)? What is his net worth?

4. What is the general partner's track record? Where can I learn more about him?

5. What type of assets will be placed in the fund, i.e., real estate, equipment, etc.?

(+) indicates favorable        (0) neutral        (−) undesirable

## TYPE: LIMITED PARTNERSHIP — RESEARCH AND DEVELOPMENT (R & D)

**DESCRIPTION** — This is perhaps one of the last ground-floor investments available today. Money is raised from investors for research and development of new inventions and ideas. As in any venture, the future returns are unknown. If the product developed and marketed becomes a success, the partners prosper quite handsomely. However, profit:loss ratios, popularity of the product, and marketing risk make this type of investment very speculative.

## FEATURES AND BENEFITS —

(−) *Degree of Safety* — Speculation on new ideas exposes investor to market risks.

(+) *Potential for Appreciation* — If your program's product does make a hit, your profits could be substantial.

(0) *Tax Benefits* — Because of extensive start-up costs, most programs provide some tax benefits.

(−) *Liquidity* — Partnerships have little or no market for partnership units.

## QUESTIONS FOR THE BROKER/INSTITUTION —

1. What is the life of the partnership?

2. What is the track record of the managing general partners?

3. What are the risks involved?

4. What are the IRS allowable tax benefits? Are tax benefits at risk of being lost to tax law changes in the near future?

(+) indicates favorable      (0) neutral      (−) undesirable

## TYPE: MORTGAGE SECURITIES

**DESCRIPTION** — With extremely high interest rates in the early 80s, financing for commercial properties and homes became extremely costly. With mortgage securities, the broker creates large packages of loans, breaks the package into smaller units, and sells them to everyday investors. The investor will receive interest and return of capital for his investment. The government also sponsors programs: the Federal Home Loan Mortgage Corporation and the Government National Mortgage Association—usually referred to as Freddie Macs, Fannie Maes, and Ginnie Maes.

## FEATURES AND BENEFITS —

(+)  *Degree of Safety* — If the security is backed by a federal agency, risk to capital is eliminated. If not, be very careful regarding the security of the investment.

(−)  *Potential for Appreciation* — They are only designed to pay interest on capital and return the capital, although profits through speculation are possible.

(−)  *Tax Benefits* — Most of these securities are fully taxable.

(0)  *Liquidity* — Depending on how the investment is structured, liquidation is usually possible.

## QUESTIONS FOR THE BROKER/INSTITUTION —

1.  Are the loans backed by the federal government? If not, how safe are they?

2.  How can I liquidate the security?

3.  How often does it pay interest? What is the tax treatment?

4.  Does the security pay me part of the profits along with interest, or does it pay interest only?

(+) indicates favorable          (0) neutral          (−) undesirable

## TYPE: MUTUAL FUNDS

**DESCRIPTION** — If ever you have desired to invest in stocks or bonds, but did not feel qualified or have the time to manage a portfolio, then mutual funds might just meet your needs. Here a group of stocks or bonds are bought and sold as a managed portfolio put together for the shareholders of the fund. Each shareholder owns shares of the mutual fund which in turn owns various stocks or bonds, depending on the fund's structure. Some funds invest strictly in common stock; others might be in bonds only; some mix and match. Each fund has its individual guideline for type of investment and strategies so potential investors have some idea of what they are buying.

## FEATURES AND BENEFITS —

(0)  *Degree of Safety* — Depends on type of fund. Ownership in a cross-section of assets gives an added degree of safety because of diversification.

(0)  *Potential for Appreciation* — Bond mutual funds are structured for income; however, stock funds offer participation in the growth market.

(0)  *Tax Benefits* — Some bond funds hold tax-free municipal bonds and provide tax-free interest.

(+)  *Liquidity* — Most investment monies can be redeemed by the fund within a couple of weeks.

## QUESTIONS FOR THE BROKER/INSTITUTION —

1.  Specifically what kind of fund is this—bonds, stocks, combinations, options, etc.?

2.  How risky is this type of fund?

3.  What is the past performance and track record of this fund, and where can I go to research this fund?

4.  What are the cost and redemption fees, if any, of liquidation?

(+) indicates favorable          (0) neutral          (−) undesirable

## TYPE: MUTUAL FUNDS — BALANCED

**DESCRIPTION** — Balanced mutual funds combine investments of various bonds and preferred and common stocks to create a fund with built-in diversification. If the market fluctuates, these funds are "guarded" because when stocks are down, bonds might be up and vice versa.

## FEATURES AND BENEFITS —

(0)  *Degree of Safety* — The bonds and preferred stocks add to the stability of the assets; however, the stocks can fluctuate with the market.

(+)  *Potential for Appreciation* — The preferred and common stocks provide potential growth.

(0)  *Tax Benefits* — Tax benefits exist for profits or losses at time of sale of the fund shares.

(+)  *Liquidity* — These fund shares can be liquidated within seven days.

## QUESTIONS FOR THE BROKER/INSTITUTION —

1.  What are the ratings of the bonds and preferred stocks?

2.  What is the history of the share value of the fund over the last few years?

3.  What kind of stocks will the fund hold?

4.  What percentage of bonds compared to stocks will be held?

(+) indicates favorable          (0) neutral          (−) undesirable

## TYPE: MUTUAL FUNDS — BOND

**DESCRIPTION** — A bond fund is a group of bonds held in a large portfolio or trust. Some funds manage the group of bonds by buying and selling when necessary or advantageous while other funds hold a group of bonds and wait for them to mature. The investors who supply the capital for the fund are called shareholders. Each shareholder owns a proportioned share of the cross-section of bonds in the fund. Some funds hold tax-exempt municipal bonds so the shareholder can receive tax-free dividends. Other funds may prefer higher, yet taxable, dividends by holding corporate and/or government bonds. In any case, the value of the bonds can rise and fall with interest rates: If the bonds or shares of the fund are sold before the bonds mature, their current interest rate could be more or less than newly-issued, competitive bonds, a phenomenon which makes your bonds or fund shares more or less attractive to new investors.

## FEATURES AND BENEFITS —

(+) *Degree of Safety* — Is high if held until bonds in fund mature; however, early redemption or sales value can fluctuate. Some funds are insured or hold only highly-rated bonds.

(–) *Potential for Appreciation* — On rare occasions, profit from speculation is possible; however, interest dividends are the only profit from this investment.

(0) *Tax Benefits* — Depends on the type of fund. Municipal bond funds provide tax-free interest; corporate and U.S. Government bond funds don't.

(+) *Liquidity* — Most bond mutual funds and trusts must redeem your shares upon request.

## QUESTIONS FOR THE BROKER/ INSTITUTION —

1. Exactly what type of bonds are held in the fund?

2. What is the rating of the individual bonds held by the fund? Where can I confirm these ratings?

3. What is the past performance of this fund? When was it established?

4. What are the costs, commissions, and fees?

(+) indicates favorable          (0) neutral          (–) undesirable

## TYPE: MUTUAL FUNDS — COMMON STOCK

**DESCRIPTION** — The mutual fund's objective can be found in the prospectus brochure, and the stated objective will let you know what type of stock the fund will purchase. The types of stock funds range from very conservative, blue-chip stock funds to more aggressive funds that hold stocks in oil, computers, small businesses, gold and silver mining. The more conservative funds will usually pay dividends.

## FEATURES AND BENEFITS —

(0) *Degree of Safety* — Compared to holding individual stocks, funds offer extensive diversification. Values can rise and fall.

(+) *Potential for Appreciation* — They can decline in value, but also have potential for appreciation, some substantially. If purchased correctly, long-term growth is likely.

(0) *Tax Benefits* — Some tax benefits are available.

(+) *Liquidity* — These funds can be redeemed at shareholder's request, but only at current market value.

## QUESTIONS FOR THE BROKER/INSTITUTION —

1. What are the objectives of the fund? What kind of stocks will it buy?

2. What is the track record of the fund and its managers?

3. If it pays income, how often?

4. What are the charges, fees, and commissions?

(+) indicates favorable          (0) neutral          (−) undesirable

## TYPE: MUTUAL FUNDS — GROWTH

**DESCRIPTION** — This type of mutual fund is designed strictly for growth and investment profit. It purchases stocks in various companies that do not pay dividends to stockholders, but re-invest profits back into the company for expansion and profitable activities. Unlike blue chip stocks or preferred stocks, the stocks held inside the growth fund are usually small, up-coming growth companies in expanding fields.

## FEATURES AND BENEFITS —

(−) *Degree of Safety* — The speculative future of the stocks increases the chances of risk.

(+) *Potential for Appreciation* — Most growth funds do very well in inflationary times. Appreciation is the primary objective of the fund.

(0) *Tax Benefits* — When profits or losses occur, the tax treatment of capital gains or losses provides desirable tax treatment.

(+) *Liquidity* — Most mutual fund shares can be liquidated within 10 days by mail.

## QUESTIONS FOR THE BROKER/INSTITUTION —

1. What is the financial stability of the companies whose stocks the fund owns?

2. What is the track record of the mutual fund and its managers?

3. In which publications are the fund's activities currently reported?

4. Are there other funds within the family of funds to transfer to if investment goals are changed? Is there a charge to reinvest dividends?

5. What purchase, transfer, and liquidation fees exist?

(+) indicates favorable      (0) neutral      (−) undesirable

139

## TYPE: MUTUAL FUNDS — INCOME

**DESCRIPTION** — Income funds are structured for maximum current income. These funds usually hold instruments such as corporate and government bonds which offer high rates of interest; they might also hold money market instruments, preferred stocks, and other interest-bearing investments. The concept is to offer high income based on long-term instruments yet remain liquid to the shareholder.

## FEATURES AND BENEFITS —

(0) *Degree of Safety* — Usually these funds remain relatively safe in principal; however, if sold on the open market, the resale or redemption value can be more or less than originally invested.

(−) *Potential for Appreciation* — Debt instruments don't appreciate unless interest rates drop below their levels.

(0) *Tax Benefits* — Most funds are taxable; however, some are comprised of tax-exempt municipal bonds.

(+) *Liquidity* — Most mutual funds can be liquidated within seven to 10 days.

## QUESTIONS FOR THE BROKER/INSTITUTION —

1. What are the ratings of the stocks or bonds in the fund?

2. What is the tax status of the fund's income return?

3. How often does the fund pay out income—quarterly? monthly?

4. What is the fund rate, and what is its track record?

(+) indicates favorable    (0) neutral    (−) undesirable

## TYPE: MUTUAL FUNDS — MONEY MARKET

**DESCRIPTION** — These funds are operated on a group-investor basis by a designated fund manager who is paid by the fund to do so. Investors send their cash to a money market fund; the money from thousands of customers is deposited, millions of dollars at a time, with various banks, government securities, or corporations to secure the highest interest rates possible. Cash is always available to the investors; in fact, most funds provide check-writing privileges with the accounts.

## FEATURES AND BENEFITS —

(+) *Degree of Safety* — The funds are usually placed with major banks, institutions, corporations, and even the U.S. Government.

(−) *Potential for Appreciation* — The principal amount, plus interest, is all that is available. No growth will occur with inflation. Interest rates are based on short-term rates.

(0) *Tax Benefits* — Most funds provide no tax benefits, and the interest earnings they provide are taxable, but there are some funds, usually with a lower yield, that pay tax-free dividends.

(+) *Liquidity* — Most funds provide limited check-writing privileges for complete liquidity.

## QUESTIONS FOR THE BROKER/INSTITUTION —

1. Where are the monies in the fund invested?

2. How safe is the fund? Is it insured or backed by secured assets?

3. How accessible is the company? Is there an 800 number I can call if I have problems?

4. Is this fund listed or rated anywhere?

(+) indicates favorable          (0) neutral          (−) undesirable

## TYPE: OIL AND GAS — GENERAL

**DESCRIPTION** — This type of investment includes the exploration, extraction, and sale of crude oil and gas reserves. There are several types of programs: buying common stocks in oil companies; oil and gas limited partnership programs. These partnerships raise monies by selling units of the partnership to investors. Then, depending on the strategy of the program, oil and gas is either searched for by the exploratory programs or purchased in the ground, then sold to oil refineries.

## FEATURES AND BENEFITS —

(0) *Degree of Safety* — Depending on the program, the drilling programs are risky; the income fund has a higher degree of safety.

(+) *Potential for Appreciation* — Oil and gas prices appreciate at very rapid rates if demand for oil increases.

(+) *Tax Benefits* — Exploration for oil provides some tax benefits at this time.

(−) *Liquidity* — Most funds last five to 12 years. Liquidation is extremely difficult.

## QUESTIONS FOR THE BROKER/INSTITUTION —

1. Exactly what type of program is this? drilling fund? income fund? balanced fund?

2. How will the program operate?

3. What is the track record of the company and its general partner?

4. What are the assets of the company and general partner?

5. What is the experience of the general partner?

(+) indicates favorable       (0) neutral       (−) undesirable

## TYPE: OIL AND GAS — DRILLING AND EXPLORATION FUNDS

**DESCRIPTION** — Drilling programs do the actual search and exploration drilling for oil and gas. These partnerships are structured so that the limited partner receives maximum tax benefits and profit potential for the risks of searching for these natural resources. These programs usually drill several wells in hopes of finding oil and gas. If only a few wells strike oil, large profits become available for investors.

### FEATURES AND BENEFITS —

(−) *Degree of Safety* — These funds are very speculative in nature.

(+) *Potential for Appreciation* — If a well produces oil or gas, high profit can exist.

(+) *Tax Benefits* — These funds offer the highest tax benefits available to oil and gas funds.

(−) *Liquidity* — The dollars in these programs are firmly committed to the exploration of oil and are expended in doing so.

### QUESTIONS FOR THE BROKER/INSTITUTION —

1. Is the fund rated anywhere? If so, how is its rate compared to others in its class?

2. Where will the fund search for oil and gas?

3. What are the tax benefits to the investor?

4. What is the fund's track record?

(+) indicates favorable          (0) neutral          (−) undesirable

## TYPE: OIL AND GAS — INCOME FUNDS

**DESCRIPTION** — This type of limited partnership investment is a long-term program structured to purchase oil and gas reserves already located in the ground. The oil and gas is extracted and resold to refineries and other customers. If the oil and gas reserves are purchased by the fund for a good price, and if oil and/or gas prices increase over the years, the investor will profit. When you purchase this investment, it will immediately begin to extract and sell the reserves. Therefore, although profits are expected, some of the income received is return of capital. The wells purchased may produce more or less than originally predicted.

## FEATURES AND BENEFITS —

(−) *Degree of Safety* — Speculation on future oil and gas prices is a risk.

(+) *Potential for Appreciation* — If good deals are made, if prices of oil and gas rise, and if more oil or gas is found near the drilling site, profits can be significant.

(0) *Tax Benefits* — Minor tax benefits exist on most funds.

(−) *Liquidity* — The oil and gas income funds are long-term programs structured for income. Some offer buy-out after two years, but most last eight to 12 years.

## QUESTIONS FOR THE BROKER/INSTITUTION —

1. Will the fund do any leveraging (borrowing) of funds?
2. What is the experience and track record of the managing general partner?
3. Where are the oil and gas-producing properties located?
4. How much income should I expect?
5. What part of my income dividends is profit, and what part is return of capital?

(+) indicates favorable        (0) neutral        (−) undesirable

## TYPE: OPTIONS

**DESCRIPTION** — An option is simply paying someone a fee or premium for the option to purchase something in the future at a predetermined price. These are called "call and put" options. They are utilized to control large amounts of assets without actually buying or selling those assets until you exercise your option. If the demand for the item agreed upon changes in value substantially, they prove quite lucrative. However, this type of investment requires careful research to fully understand your true position. They are extremely risky. Loss of principal should be expected on some of the transactions.

## FEATURES AND BENEFITS —

(−)  *Degree of Safety* — Buying options is very risky because the market must move substantially in your direction to allow profit.

(+)  *Potential for Appreciation* — If in fact you are fortunate to have the market in your favor, an option can multiply; you gain.

(0)  *Tax Benefits* — There are tax rules that apply strictly to options. However, options are traded strictly for profit.

(+)  *Liquidity* — They can be traded on an open "options" market.

## QUESTIONS FOR THE BROKER/INSTITUTION —

1.  How is this option structured? Am I buying or selling the option?

2.  Where is the option traded?

3.  How much does the market have to move before I make any money? And in which direction?

4.  When does this option expire?

(+) indicates favorable          (0) neutral          (−) undesirable

## TYPE: REAL ESTATE — ACTUAL STRUCTURES

**DESCRIPTION** — This investment comes in many forms for the investor, such as personal residence, rental property, apartment buildings, office buildings, etc.

## FEATURES AND BENEFITS —

(0) *Degree of Safety* — If you buy a home, the investment is relatively safe as long as you can pay the mortgage or pay cash.

(+) *Potential for Appreciation* — When inflation occurs, the cost of building new homes increases. This increases the value of existing real estate.

(+) *Tax Benefits* — At present, there are various tax benefits: interest deductions, depreciation allowance on rental property, etc.

(−) *Liquidity* — You must find a buyer. Many times the assistance of a real estate broker is required.

## QUESTIONS FOR THE BROKER/INSTITUTION —

1. What is the average price of building in the area?

2. What are the zonings in the area?

3. What are the terms of the financing?

4. How strong is the economic base in the area, and what are the vacancy levels?

(+) indicates favorable          (0) neutral          (−) undesirable

## TYPE: REAL ESTATE — INVESTMENT TRUSTS (REITs)

**DESCRIPTION** — REITs are structured much like the mutual fund. The REIT owns a cross-section of real estate properties and/or income-producing mortgages. The investor purchases shares of the trust which represent ownership in several properties and/or mortgages. These trusts appreciate and usually produce income as well. They can be liquidated if necessary. Some are even sold like stock on the "over-the-counter" market.

## FEATURES AND BENEFITS —

(0)  *Degree of Safety* — Most have a fairly high degree of safety based on all cash or on mortgages backed by real estate.

(+)  *Potential for Appreciation* — The potential for real estate to rise in value with inflation is good.

(0)  *Tax Benefits* — Income is offset to some extent by tax benefits like depreciation.

(+)  *Liquidity* — Most REITs can be liquidated on the open market or sold to a market maker.

## QUESTIONS FOR THE BROKER/INSTITUTION —

1.  What assets are placed in the fund? Is it all real estate or does it hold mortgages?

2.  How do I sell this investment if I need to?

3.  What is the program's track record?

4.  Is there any pay-out dividends? And if so, how often?

5.  What tax benefits, if any, are available?

(+) indicates favorable          (0) neutral          (−) undesirable

## TYPE: REAL ESTATE — LIMITED PARTNERSHIPS

**DESCRIPTION** — Although these programs vary drastically in their structure and guidelines, the basics remain the same. They raise funds to purchase properties, manage the properties, and in a few to several years sell them. The limited partner (the investor) has limited liability and is only at risk for the amount invested. The managing general partner is allowed to take some of the profits when properties are sold. The limited partners keep the primary profits and tax benefits.

## FEATURES AND BENEFITS —

(0) *Degree of Safety* — Depends on the structure of the program. More risks exist if extensive borrowing is done.

(+) *Potential for Appreciation* — Real estate has historically appreciated over the years.

(+) *Tax Benefits* — Interest expenses, depreciations, and other tax benefits exist.

(−) *Liquidity* — Most programs cannot be prematurely liquidated.

## QUESTIONS FOR THE BROKER/INSTITUTION —

1. How is the partnership structured? What are the objectives?

2. Is there going to be borrowing of funds internally? If so, to what extent?

3. What is the managing general partner's track record?

4. How long is the life of the partnership, and will it sell for all cash or take back loans from the time the properties are sold?

(+) indicates favorable     (0) neutral     (−) undesirable

## TYPE: REAL ESTATE — LIMITED PARTNERSHIP DEVELOPMENT FUNDS

**DESCRIPTION** — The development of real estate requires funds that can be invested without need for cash flow. These programs purchase land with the intention of doing the actual construction on the properties. Some funds will purchase properties from distressed builders and do the completion. Some programs purchase raw land. After receiving favorable zoning to build, they either go ahead and build the structures or sell the property at a profit from zoning improvements.

### FEATURES AND BENEFITS —

(−) *Degree of Safety* — These programs involve certain degrees of speculation due to unknown rent factors and resale profits. Also, zoning and city regulations can slow progress down.

(+) *Potential for Appreciation* — If successful, these funds can do quite well if managed properly.

(0) *Tax Benefits* — Vary because of building expenses and different degrees of leverage.

(−) *Liquidity* — They are extremely difficult to liquidate.

### QUESTIONS FOR THE BROKER/INSTITUTION —

1. Where will properties be bought or built?

2. How much leverage (borrowing) will occur?

3. What is the general partner's track record?

4. When will properties be sold?

(+) indicates favorable       (0) neutral       (−) undesirable

## TYPE: REAL ESTATE — LIMITED PARTNERSHIP GROWTH FUNDS

**DESCRIPTION** — This type of program is usually structured for maximum growth potential which is accomplished by the use of aggressive purchasing methods, including medium to high levels of leverage. Leverage is the practice of investing a certain amount of funds and borrowing the balance on a mortgage. This practice allows the purchase of greater amounts of property than dollars committed. If property values increase, these funds perform quite well. In addition, larger tax benefits exist because the investor receives tax benefits on the full value of real estate purchased by the fund regardless of the amount of money the partnership actually put up. However, this kind of investment requires close management to insure profitability.

## FEATURES AND BENEFITS —

(0)  *Degree of Safety* — Depends on levels of leverage and speculation. These funds should be reviewed closely to insure proper precautions, structure, and management are being practiced.

(+)  *Potential for Appreciation* — Because leverage allows multiple growth of the original funds invested, these funds have great potential for growth if real estate increases in value.

(+)  *Tax Benefits* — The leverage factor increases tax benefits by multiplying amounts of tax deductions by leverage ratios.

(−)  *Liquidity* — Few funds provide liquidity. You should expect to be committed for an excess of five years.

## QUESTIONS FOR THE BROKER/INSTITUTION —

1.  What degree of leverage will be utilized by the fund, and what are the financing risks?

2.  Where are the properties located?

3.  What is the economic stability of the general partner, and has he ever lost property or been named in a civil suit?

4.  What is the track record of the fund manager or of prior funds?

(+) indicates favorable      (0) neutral      (−) undesirable

## TYPE: REAL ESTATE — LIMITED PARTNERSHIP INCOME FUNDS

**DESCRIPTION** — This real estate partnership is usually structured to produce current income for the investor. Properties purchased for the fund are usually paid for by an all-cash purchase. This allows the partnership to be free of any debt. These funds usually purchase properties that are already occupied by tenants who will sign or have already signed long-term leases. This practice allows the fund to pay out all of the rental income after expenses to the limited partners on a consistent basis. The limited partner receives a good rate of income yet has growth potential in the increase in market value of the properties.

**FEATURES AND BENEFITS** —

(0)   *Degree of Safety* — Properties are held free and clear. Some risk exists in a fluctuating market. However, this is one of the most conservative methods of holding real estate.

(+)   *Potential for Appreciation* — Historically, real estate, if purchased, managed, and maintained properly, has appreciated very significantly in the U.S.

(+)   *Tax Benefits* — Some of the income is offset by depreciation of the buildings in the fund.

(−)   *Liquidity* — These funds must invest your money into real estate and leave it there for a while. Short of a family emergency, you can't get it out until the fund sells off the properties.

**QUESTIONS FOR THE BROKER/INSTITUTION** —

1.   What type of properties will be purchased by the fund, and where will they be located?

2.   What is the life of the fund?

3.   How soon will the income begin, and how is it paid?

4.   How long has the general partner been in the business, and what is his track record?

(+) indicates favorable          (0) neutral          (−) undesirable

## TYPE: RETIREMENT INVESTMENTS — INDIVIDUAL RETIREMENT ACCOUNTS (IRAs)

**DESCRIPTION** — This is not actually an investment in itself; it is merely a designation for certain funds you choose to claim as an investment for retirement. Because the social security program, as we know it today, is not intended to provide full retirement benefits, Congress was concerned about encouraging people to become self-sufficient at retirement. The funds placed into or designated as IRA funds are tax deductible from the year's income, allowing a significant reduction in taxes. Certain limits do exist, however, on the amount of contribution and the age at which you withdraw funds.

### FEATURES AND BENEFITS —

(+) *Degree of Safety* — If invested wisely, the IRA can take on any level of safety desired.

(+) *Potential for Appreciation* — Depending on the investments making up the IRA funding, these funds can grow significantly—especially since they are tax sheltered and can grow without taxation.

(+) *Tax Benefits* — All funds contributed are tax deductible and can accumulate tax free until withdrawal.

(−) *Liquidity* — By law, there is a penalty to withdraw. Also, the funds are treated as taxable income in the year they are withdrawn. No penalty applies if you reach retirement age or become legally disabled.

### QUESTIONS FOR THE BROKER/INSTITUTION —

1. What are the set-up costs and yearly fees?

2. Are there transaction fees? Do I pay more if I add more investments to the IRA account?

3. When do I get the IRA reports informing me of the account?

4. Can this IRA purchase an investment for me, or is it limited to one company's or bank's instruments?

(+) indicates favorable        (0) neutral        (−) undesirable

## TYPE: RETIREMENT INVESTMENTS — PENSION/PROFIT-SHARING PLANS

**DESCRIPTION** — This is a form of retirement plan for owners and employees of various businesses and companies. The pension plan is a predesignated plan which requires continuous contributions annually. The profit-sharing plan, on the other hand, is only contributed to if profit exists at the end of the year; contributions are not required.

**FEATURES AND BENEFITS —**

(+)  *Degree of Safety* — Depending on where funds are invested, safety can be easily achieved.

(+)  *Potential for Appreciation* — Appreciation depends on specific investments placed into the plans.

(+)  *Tax Benefits* — Usually there is a 100% tax deduction on all contributions going into the plan.

(0)  *Liquidity* — It can be liquidated; however, there are penalties on all early withdrawals, some provide loan features.

**QUESTIONS FOR THE BROKER/INSTITUTION —**

1.  What are the administrative fees for the plan?

2.  What options do I have for investment alternatives for the plan's funds?

3.  What age must I be or for what reasons may I withdraw my funds?

4.  Can I borrow these funds in the future?

(+) indicates favorable      (0) neutral      (−) undesirable

## TYPE: STOCKS — ADJUSTABLE RATE PREFERRED

**DESCRIPTION** — A preferred stock whose dividend is adjusted each quarter so that the dividend reflects the market. The rates fluctuate with the prevailing money market rates; however, they are preferred stocks, not bonds. The adjusting dividend rates are meant to stabilize the asset value.

## FEATURES AND BENEFITS —

(0)  *Degree of Safety* — The adjusting rates are designed to keep the price as stable as possible.

(+)  *Potential for Appreciation* — There is potential for appreciation if the company improves dramatically and the stock price increases.

(−)  *Tax Benefits* — Tax benefits are minor; whereas, they used to be significant.

(+)  *Liquidity* — They can be sold on the open market.

## QUESTIONS FOR THE BROKER/INSTITUTION —

1.  What is the current tax status to corporations and the dividends they earn?

2.  What is the rating or status of the preferred?

3.  What is the track record of dividends of the issuing company?

4.  What is the current and expected dividend?

5.  Where is the stock listed? What stock exchange?

(+) indicates favorable          (0) neutral          (−) undesirable

## TYPE: STOCKS — COMMON

**DESCRIPTION** — A form of ownership in a company or business that does not require additional involvement other than the purchase of the stock shares themselves. The stock shares represent the holder's ownership in the company. When there are company profits, the stock holder is entitled to those profits. There is no personal risk of owning the shares. However, the value of the company and its stock shares can increase or decrease in value. Where the actual company may be worth one amount depending on the market, the stock may be selling for much more or much less than that, thus creating some speculation in its actual value.

## FEATURES AND BENEFITS —

(0)  *Degree of Safety* — Varies with the different types of stocks. Preferred and blue chip stock is considered fairly safe whereas growth stocks are speculative.

(+)  *Potential for Appreciation* — Many stocks have tended to follow inflationary trends. Some have increased substantially, but the reverse is always possible.

(0)  *Tax Benefits* — Some tax benefits are available to the holder of stock when selling.

(+)  *Liquidity* — Most stocks have a market in which they can be sold.

## QUESTIONS FOR THE BROKER/INSTITUTION —

1.  What is the specific classification of this stock—preferred, blue chip, growth, etc.?

2.  Where is the stock traded?

3.  What is the track record or history of the company and the stock itself?

4.  Where can I get independent literature regarding this and other stock, such as stock ratings, etc.?

(+) indicates favorable        (0) neutral        (−) undesirable

## TYPE: TREASURY BILLS (T-BILLS)

**DESCRIPTION** — T-bills are short-term notes issued by the federal government with maturity dates of three months, six months, and 12 months. They are available in $5,000 multiples after the $10,000 minimum is met. This investment is free of any credit risk. If the U.S. Government has financial problems, it can simply print more money. However, the printing affects the value of the dollar, causing it to buy less and less in the open market. Federal reserve banks and branches can issue T-bills, and many money market mutual funds hold multiples of treasury bills for the investor. T-bills are sold at a discount and later mature at face value.

## FEATURES AND BENEFITS —

(+) *Degree of Safety* — This instrument is backed by the U.S. Government. The treasury has the ability to print more money when necessary, a practice which can cause inflation.

(−) *Potential for Appreciation* — You will only receive interest accrued. The principal is paid back at the purchase amount.

(0) *Tax Benefits* — T-bill interest is exempt from many state taxes. However, the interest earned by lending to the government is not tax exempt at the federal level.

(−) *Liquidity* — You must wait until the maturity date of your T-bill before you will receive the principal and interest.

## QUESTIONS FOR THE BROKER/INSTITUTION —

1. What is the exact length of maturity?

2. Are there any charges to me on the purchase?

3. How do I sell the T-bill if I need cash, or can I borrow against it?

(+) indicates favorable      (0) neutral      (−) undesirable

# GLOSSARY

## A

ABOVE PAR — the price of a stock or bond that is higher than its value.

ACCELERATED DEPRECIATION — depreciation at a greater than expected rate.

ACCELERATION CLAUSE — a clause included in the contract stipulating the entire balance shall become due and payable in the event of a breach of contract.

ACCIDENTAL DEATH BENEFIT — amount payable to the beneficiary, plus the face amount of the insurance policy, in the event of an accidental death.

ACCIDENT AND HEALTH INSURANCE — a type of coverage that pays benefits in case of sickness, accidental injury, or accidental death, and sometimes including reimbursement for loss of income.

ACCIDENT INSURANCE — insurance against a disabling accident that renders the insured from earning an income.

ACCOUNT BALANCE — the net debit or net credit amount in a specific account in the ledger.

ACCOUNT IN TRUST — an account opened for another person to be held in trust by a different person.

ACCOUNTS PAYABLE — an amount owed by a business or individual to a creditor for merchandise or services purchased.

ACCOUNTS RECEIVABLE — money owed to a business for merchandise purchased on account.

ACCRUE — to accumulate.

ACCRUED CHARGES — charges that are not yet due.

ACCRUED DIVIDEND — regular dividend considered to be earned but not declared or payable on legally issued stock of a legally organized business.

ACCRUED EXPENSES — when a business has used goods or services provided before it has paid for them.

ACCRUED INTEREST PAYABLE — interest accumulated on a debt but not yet paid.

ACCRUED INTEREST RECEIVABLE — interest earned by a bank that has not been collected.

ACCRUED LIABILITIES — liabilities that have not been paid as a result of expenses that have been incurred.

ACCUMULATION DIVIDEND — a dividend that has not been paid when it was due.

ACCELERATED DEPRECIATION — an accounting practice affecting taxable or net income in which initially large sums that diminish annually are charged off.

ACID-TEST RATIO — a credit barometer used to indicate the ability of a business enterprise to meet its current obligations.

ACQUISITION — the taking over of one company by another.

ACRE — used to measure land. One acre equals 4840 square yards.

ACT OF GOD — an accident by natural causes that could not be prevented by reasonable foresight or care.

ACTUAL CASH VALUE — the cost of replacing damaged property with like kind and quality in the same physical condition.

ACTUARY — an individual who determines reserves against future liabilities for corporate and rate-making.

ADJUSTABLE RATE MORTGAGES ("ARMS") — a type of mortgage loan used for financing home purchases and other major items. The reason for such a loan is to decrease the loan rate. The bank rides with the market and raises rates if necessary.

ADJUSTED GROSS INCOME — the income of an individual minus expenses.

AGENT — insurance: an individual who represents insurance companies.

ALL-INCLUSIVE CONCEPT — an income statement incorporating all items of revenue and expense in computing net income for an accounting period.

ALL-RISK LEVERAGE — a type of insurance coverage that protects against all dangers or hazards that might befall what is being insured unless specifically excluded in the contract.

ALL-SAVERS' CERTIFICATES — a tax break created under the Economic Recovery Tax Act of 1981 to encourage savings.

AMENITY — features that make property more attractive.

AMERICAN DEPOSITORY RECEIPT (ADR) — a negotiable share in some of the stocks or bonds a foreign issuer may have in trust, held by an American bank.

AMERICAN STOCK EXCHANGE — the world's second largest stock exchange.

AMEX COMMODITIES EXCHANGE (ACE) — a commodities exchange, launched by the American Stock Exchange, that offers its member firms a broader range of products.

AMORTIZATION— resolving a debt, usually through periodic installment payments.

ANNUAL PERCENTAGE RATE (APR) — the basic finance or service charges on a loan.

# GLOSSARY

**ANNUAL REPORT** — a report of financial conditions prepared at yearly intervals.

**ANNUITANT** — the person who receives annuity payments.

**ANNUITY** — a contract with an insurance company which guarantees periodic payments to an individual for either a specified number of years or life.

**ANNUITY ACCUMULATION PERIOD** — the time span in which an individual makes a deposit in his retirement fund before the annuity payments begin.

**ANNUITY ACCUMULATION UNIT** — an accounting method used to determine the value of an individual's accumulation account before the annuity payments begin.

**ANNUITY ACCUMULATION VALUE** — the number of accumulation units credited to the account of a variable annuity contract holder.

**ANNUITY COMMENCEMENT DATE** — the day on which annuity payments begin.

**ANNUITY PERIOD** — the period after retirement during which an annuitant receives payments.

**ANTICIPATED INTEREST** — the projected amount of interest on a savings account.

**APPRAISAL** — a formal estimate of value of an asset.

**APPRECIATION** — an increase over time of the dollar value of a given asset.

**ARBITRAGE** — a practice of buying products on one exchange and selling them on another exchange with the hopes of buying in one exchange for less and selling for more on the other exchange.

**ASSET VALUE** — the total of an investment company's cash plus the market value of its securities minus its total liabilities (also net asset value).

**ASSETS** — all types of property owned by an individual or a business.

**ASSUMPTION** — accepted bank loan payments by a party other than the original maker.

**"AT THE MARKET"** — used in describing buy or sell orders for securities at the best going price in the market.

**AUDIT** — an official inspection to check the accuracy of figures and statements in a tax return or account book.

**AUTOMATIC REINVESTMENT PLAN** — an option offered by a mutual fund in which all cash dividends and capital gains' distributions are reinvested for additional shares of the fund rather than disbursed to the investor.

## B

**BALANCE SHEET** — an itemized statement of total assets and liabilities of a business.

BALANCED MUTUAL FUND — balancing various proportions of bonds, preferred stocks, and common stocks to maintain greater stability of both capital and income.

BALLOON CLAUSE (or payment) — a clause in a loan contract which calls for a final payment which is much larger than earlier payments on the loan. This payment terminates debt.

BANKER'S ACCEPTANCE — an acceptance by a bank of a draft drawn on behalf of a customer which becomes equivalent to a promissory note of the bank, usually payable within 90 days.

BANKRUPTCY — the conditions under which the financial position of an individual or business causes legal insolvency or lack of funds.

BASIS POINT — used in quoting bond and money market yields equivalent to one one-hundredth of a percentage point.

BEAR MARKET — a term used to denote a downward price trend in the securities market.

BEARER BONDS — bonds which are sold with coupons denoting amount of interest to be paid to the bearer of these coupons. The investor detaches the coupons and delivers them to a specified bank where they will be exchanged for cash.

BENEFICIARY — a person stated in a will, trust, or life insurance contract that receives certain benefits.

BEQUEST — a gift of personal property made by an individual.

BID AND ASK — a bid is a proposal to buy at a specific price. An ask is a corresponding offer to sell at a specific price.

BIG EIGHT — Arthur Andersen and Company; Coopers and Lybrand; Ernst and Ernst; Haskins and Sells; Peat, Marwick, Mitchell and Company; Price Waterhouse and Company; Touche Ross and Company; and Arthur Young and Company are the largest public accounting firms.

BLANKET POLICY — rather than covering separate items under an insurance policy, this policy covers several different properties, shipments, or locations under one item.

BLUE-CHIP STOCKS — common stock of large corporations which are well known and financially strong and have a good record of earnings and dividend payments over a number of years.

BLUE SKY LAW — a term used to prevent fraud in securities sales and disposition.

BODILY INJURY LIABILITY INSURANCE — protection against loss from damages of bodily injury, sickness, or disease sustained by any person other than the employees of the insured.

BOND INDENTURE — the contract of a corporate bond which tells of the complete rights and duties of the three parties of the contract: the corporation, the trustee, and the bondholders.

BOND ISSUE — the entire group of similar bonds sold under the same indenture.

# GLOSSARY

**BOND (YIELD) TABLE** — a table which shows the various yields on a bond given its interest rate and its capital gain or loss at maturity (when bought at various prices).

**BONDS** — an interest-bearing certificate of debt.

**BOOK VALUE** — the known cost price of a security less depreciation or other write-downs. The value of a share is equal to assets minus liabilities divided by the number of shares outstanding.

**BROKER** — an individual who executes transactions in securities for others.

**BROKER DEALER** — a securities dealer who serves not only as a broker but as a trader of principle with customers.

**BULL MARKET** — a term used to denote an upward price trend in the securities market.

**BULLION** — formed in ingots or bars for use in coinage, usually gold or silver.

## C

**CALL OPTION** — a contract in which the purchaser has the option to buy a given stock at a given price within a specific period of time.

**CALLABLE BOND** — a bond issue, all or part of which may be redeemed before maturity by the issuing corporation under definite conditions.

**CAPITAL** — total assets less total liabilities. Often regarded as an accumulation of goods for consumption or production.

**CAPITAL ASSETS** — includes fixed assets as differentiated from property consumed and property that yields income.

**CAPITAL GAINS** — the gain resulting when the selling price of an asset is more than the cost of that asset.

**CAPITAL GAINS TAXES** — the specific tax rate at which capital gains are taxed.

**CAPITAL INVESTMENTS** — funds invested in assets that are not expected to be returned during the normal course of business in the coming fiscal period.

**CAPITAL LOSS** — the loss which results from a decline in the value of an asset.

**CAPITAL STRUCTURE** — the proportions of capital represented by various securities, bonds, preferred stock, and common stock.

**CAPITALIZE** — to convert into cash that which can be used in production.

**CARRY-OVER** — the amount of a taxpayer's loss that was not absorbed as carry-back and may be deducted off taxable income of succeeding years (in federal income taxes).

**CASH ACCOUNTING** — an accounting system whereby revenues are accounted for and entered only when money is received.

**CASH FLOW** — the cash receipts from operations in excess of operating expenses. A rough measure of profitability.

CASH ON DELIVERY (COD) — terms of sale wherein the invoice is due and payable before the merchandise is released from shipment.

CASH SURRENDER VALUE — the sum total of money paid by an insurance company upon cancellation of a policy.

CERTIFICATE OF DEPOSIT — the CD, as most of us call it, is basically a "time deposit" or a deposit of money that you, the customer, place with the bank. The agreement with the bank is that it keeps your money for a specified period of time, lending it out for higher and longer term rates. You in turn receive higher interest rates for tying your funds up for periods of 30, 60, 90 days and longer, but cannot liquidate the funds without penalty.

CERTIFICATE OF INSURANCE — evidence that an insurance policy has been issued.

CHURNING — the repetitive buying and selling of securities when such activity has a minimal effect on the market but generates additional commissions to a stock broker.

CLOSED-END FUNDS — this term is usually used in conjunction with mutual funds that pool monies together for mutual investments. This type of fund raises a specified amount of monies in order to purchase stocks, bonds, etc. and, after reaching the desired amount, closes its doors to new investors. The only way to buy in after the primary issue is on the open market on a resale basis.

CO-INSURANCE — a provision in a policy that requires that the insured carry additional insurance equal to a certain specified percentage of the value of the property.

COLLECTIBLES — these investments range from fine art, paintings, coins, to antique automobiles and other items that bring higher prices than the original price.

COLLISION INSURANCE — this is coverage for damage to the insured caused by collision with any object, either stationary or moving.

COMMERCIAL BANK — specializes in demand deposits and commercial loans.

COMMERCIAL PAPER — corporate debt maturing in 270 days or less which is sold primarily to banks and other short-term investors.

COMMISSION BROKERAGE — brokers whose income mainly consists of commissions obtained by buying and selling securities for their customers.

COMMON STOCK EQUITIES — the basic certificate of ownership in a corporation. Issued by corporations to raise capital and traded among investors at market prices.

COMMUNITY PROPERTY — property that is jointly owned by a husband and wife.

CONSEQUENTIAL LOSS — loss occurring because of physical damage to property.

CONSUMER PRICE INDEX — a device by which the increase or the cost of living is measured. Usually taken as a general measure of the amount of inflation which has taken place.

CONTRIBUTORY PENSION PLAN — when an employer and employee jointly finance a pension plan.

CONTROL STOCK — securities belonging to those who have controlling interest in a company.

CONVERTIBLE BOND — a security issued by a company which is convertible to an amount of common stock upon the holder's option.

CONVEYANCE — when ownership of property is passed from one person or organization to another by a deed.

COOLING-OFF PERIOD — finance: a period of time that must elapse before the filing of a registration for a new security and public sale.

COST-OF-LIVING INDEX — a measurement of changes in prices of goods and services purchased by moderate-income families.

COUPON BOND — a bond containing coupons which represent interest payments accrued on the bond. These coupons are collectible like checks when due.

CREDIT LIABILITIES — the outstanding debts of an individual which must be paid off within one year. Includes bank loans and accrued taxes.

CREDIT UNION — a group of individuals, state or federally chartered, who collect deposits from its members in order to obtain loans for its members.

CUMULATIVE PREFERRED (STOCK) — a stock whose holders are entitled to be paid on the omitted dividends before dividends are paid on the company's common stock.

CURRENCY DEPRECIATION — decline in the value of a national currency under a flexible exchange rate system.

CURRENT ASSETS — the assets of an individual which can normally be converted into cash within one year. Includes cash, receivables, and other highly liquid holdings.

CURRENT DOLLARS — the actual prices of goods and services each year.

CURRENT LIABILITIES — money owed and payable by a company within one year.

CURRENT RATIO — the ratio of current assets to current liabilities. This ratio shows the financial soundness of a business or individual.

## D

DAY ORDER — an order to buy or sell that expires at the end of the trading day on which it was entered.

DEALER — in the securities business, an individual or firm acting as a principal rather than an agent.

DEBENTURE — a bond which is secured by no specific assets but by the credit and all assets of the corporation.

DEBIT CARD — a computerized innovation that permits bank customers to withdraw cash from any affiliated automated teller machine and to make cashless purchases from funds on deposit without incurring revolving finance charges for credit.

DECLARATION — a statement by an applicant for insurance. This is copied into the policy.

DEED — a written agreement of transfer by which title to an estate or other real property is transmitted from one person to another.

DEED OF TRUST — when a third party is entrusted to ensure payment of the indebtedness or to ensure that other conditions of the transaction are met.

DEFAULT — the failure to meet the terms of a contract. Usually has to do with the failure to pay bonds or shares of stock.

DEFAULT CLAUSE — an agreement in a lease which defines the rights of the parties upon the default.

DEFENSIVE INVESTMENT — an investment practice that attempts to reduce both the risk of loss and the need for special knowledge, skill, and continuous attention.

DEFENSIVE STOCK — a stock whose price is unlikely to decline with the market due to the strength and nature of the business it represents.

DEFERRED ANNUITY — an annuity contract that provides for the postponement of the start of an annuity until after a specified period or until the annuitant attains a specified age.

DEFERRED SALE CONTRACT — when a purchaser pays the owner all or part of the sale price of a property through an obligation other than cash by contract.

DEFICIT FINANCING — making up the differences by borrowing.

DEFICIT SPENDING — the spending of public funds raised by borrowing rather than by taxation.

DEPENDENTS — relatives or non-relatives receiving more than half of their support from a taxpayer.

DEPRECIATION — charges against earnings to write off the cost of an asset over its estimated useful life less salvage value.

DEPRECIATION BASE — the amount that the IRS recognizes as depreciable on a property's improvements.

DILUTION — the act of issuing more securities, thus reducing actual earnings or asset coverage per bond or share of stock.

DISABILITY INCOME — a specific health insurance contract, which is provided by a benefit, that indemnifies the insured for loss of time in the event of sickness or accident.

DISCOUNT — sold at less than face value. With time passage, security value rises to reflect accrued interest.

DISCOUNT BOND — the difference between the face value and the sale price of a bond when it is sold below its face value.

**DISCOUNT RATE** — an interest rate used in evaluating expenditures that measures the relative value of benefits or returns obtained now (charged by the Federal Reserve System to its members).

**DIVERSIFICATION** — the purchase of varying assets in order to minimize the risk associated with a portfolio.

**DIVEST** — to remove a vested right.

**DIVIDEND** — a distribution of the profits of a corporation made to the stockholders on a "per share" basis.

**DIVIDEND PAYOUT RATIO** — dividends per share of common stock to earnings per share of common stock.

**DOLLAR-COST AVERAGING** — buying securities in uniform sums at intervals in a downward market to lower the average price of the securities.

**DOW JONES AVERAGES** — a device used to measure the general trends in the market prices of various securities.

## E

**EARNED INCOME** — income derived from goods and services rendered.

**EARNEST MONEY** — money given by a contracting party at the time of the signing of a contract to bind the contract.

**EARNINGS PER SHARE** — the earning of a corporation for a stated period, dividend by the number of shares of common stock outstanding during this stated period.

**EARNINGS YIELD** — the earnings per share, expressed as a percentage of stock price.

**EASEMENT** — a limited right to use someone else's property.

**ECONOMIC RENT** — a rent that a certain building would command at a given point in time, usually during an appraisal.

**EMPLOYEE RETIREMENT INCOME SECURITY ACT OF 1974 (ERISA)** — legislation signed to protect the interests of workers who participate in private pension and welfare plans and their beneficiaries (signed by President Ford).

**EMPLOYEE STOCK OWNERSHIP PLANS (ESOPs)** — programs that are created so employees feel they have participation in the management and direction of a company.

**ENCUMBRANCE** — a provision which affects the title to a property (mortgages, restrictions, easements, liens).

**ENDOWMENT INSURANCE** — a life insurance on which premiums are paid for when the insured is covered. When a set date is met, no further premiums are required.

**ENTREPRENEUR** — a person who assumes the undertaking of a business and its financial risk as well as its operation and management.

EQUIPMENT LEASING — the process of renting expensive equipment to save immediate cash outlay.

EQUIPMENT TRUST CERTIFICATE — a type of security usually issued by a railroad to pay for new equipment.

EQUITY CAPITAL — investments made in an organization by stockholders or owners.

EQUITY FINANCING — selling of capital stock by a corporation.

EQUITY SECURITIES — any stock issue, common or preferred.

ERRORS AND OMISSIONS — insurance coverage for liability arising out of errors or omissions in the performance of professional services.

ESCALATOR CLAUSE — in the event of unforeseen occurrences, this contract clause provides for increased payments.

ESCAPE CLAUSE — a clause in a lease allowing the lease to be terminated before the contract expires. Penalty terms and several months notice are required.

ESCROW — in the process of the sale of real property, a third party holds deposits of all monies, contracts, mortgages, and deeds until the sale is finalized. The third party will then distribute all monies and papers as directed.

ESTATE — all assets owned by an individual at the time of his or her death.

ESTATE PLANNING — planning assets, bequests, and estate disposition to assure liquidity, provide for family needs, minimize confusion, and avoid unnecessary taxes and forced sales.

ESTATE TAX — a state or federal excise tax placed on an estate, to be paid before property is transferred to heirs.

ESTATE TAX PRIVILEGE — a tax privilege attached to certain long-term government bonds allowing these bonds to be cashed at principal in order to pay estate taxes.

ESTATE TAXES — a tax levied by the government which is based on the total size of the descendents' taxable estate.

EURODOLLAR — dollar deposits in banks outside the United States.

EX-DIVIDEND — when a stock is sold ex-dividend, the seller retains the pending dividend.

EXCLUSIVE LISTING — when a broker becomes the sole agent of the owner of a property.

EXECUTOR — a person identified in a will to administer the estate upon the death of the testator.

EXECUTRIX — a woman identified in a will to administer the estate upon the death of the testator.

## F

FACE VALUE — the principal value of a note or bond on which interest is computed for interest-bearing obligations.

FEDERAL AGENCY BONDS — bonds issued by government agencies, e.g., Federal Land Bank, FNMA, GNMA. These carry higher yield and risk than government bonds.

FEDERAL DEPOSIT INSURANCE CORPORATION — a government corporation that insures the deposits of all banks that are entitled to the benefits of insurance under the Federal Reserve Act.

FEDERAL HOUSING ADMINISTRATION (FHA) — promotes the ownership of homes and also the renovation and remodeling of residences through government-guaranteed loans to home owners.

FEDERAL LOAN BANKS — banks (12) established in 1916 to make available long-term mortgage loans to farmers to enable them to own their own farms.

FEDERAL NATIONAL MORTGAGE ASSOCIATION (FNMA) — an independent agency whose major function is to purchase mortgages from banks, trust companies, mortgage companies, savings and loan associations, and insurance companies to help these institutions with their distribution of funds for home mortgages (Fannie Mae).

FEDERAL RESERVE BANK — one of the 12 banks created by and operating under the Federal Reserve System.

FEDERAL RESERVE BOARD — the seven-member governing body of the Federal Reserve System.

FEDERAL SAVINGS AND LOAN ASSOCIATION — one of the associations established by the Home Owners' Loan Act of 1934 which brought existing and newly formed mutual savings banks and building and loan associations under a federal charter.

FEDERAL SECURITIES ACTS — major laws and amendments which regulate the securities business.

FIDUCIARY — an individual who holds certain financial rights, powers, and responsibilities for another person's benefit.

FINANCIAL LEVERAGE — fixed return elements in the financial structure of a company. Profits may not be proportional to revenues.

FINANCIAL STATEMENT — any statement made by an individual, a proprietorship, a partnership, a corporation, an organization, or an association regarding its financial status.

FIRST LIEN — a first mortgage.

FIXED ANNUITY — a life insurance contract that insures fixed, periodic payments for life or for a specified time period.

FIXED ASSETS — long-term business assets which include land, buildings, and machinery.

FLOATER POLICY — a policy under whose terms protection follows movable property, covering it wherever it may be.

FROZEN ASSET — any asset that cannot be used by its owner because of pending or on-going legal action.

FROZEN PENSION — a pension that is paid in full. The pension that is given an employee when he leaves the company.

# G

GENERAL OBLIGATION (G.O.) — a municipal or state bond which carries an unconditional obligation to pay and is issued by a governmental body that has the power to levy taxes.

GIFT TAXES — taxes levied by federal government and some states on donors of non-charitable gifts.

GOODWILL — the intangible possession that enables a business to continue to earn profit in excess of the normal or basic rate of profit earned by other businesses of similar type.

GOVERNMENT BOND — an obligation of the U.S. Government.

GRACE PERIOD — the amount of time after the due date that the premium of life insurance policy may be paid without additional penalty, usually 30 days.

GRADUATED PAYMENT MORTGAGE — a type of mortgage that provides lower initial monthly payments than a standard mortgage. Mortgage payments and the outstanding principal increase gradually during the early years for a certain period.

GROSS INCOME — revenues before any expenses have been deducted.

GROUP INSURANCE — an insurance plan entered into jointly with others, usually procured and subsidized by an employer.

GROWTH STOCK — a stock that has shown in the past and is expected to show in the future better than average earnings' growth (i.e., its appreciation in the market price is better than average).

GUARANTEED BOND — a bond where the principal and interest payments are guaranteed by a firm separate from the issuer.

# H

HEALTH INSURANCE — insurance that provides indemnity for loss of time and for medical expenses due to sickness.

HEDGE — an investment made opposite of another investment in order to reduce the risk of the investment.

HOSPITALIZATION INSURANCE — insurance that provides indemnity for hospital, nursing, surgical, and miscellaneous medical expenses resulting from bodily injury or illness.

HYPOTHECATE — to promise and place property to secure a loan.

HYPOTHECATION — the pledging of securities as collateral.

**I**

ILLIQUID — finance: not easily convertible into cash.

IN THE BLACK — describing a business that is functioning with a profit.

IN THE MONEY — a call option in which the striking price is below the market price of the underlying stock.

IN THE RED — describing a business that is functioning with a loss.

INCOME BONDS — bonds which pay interest only when income is earned.

INCOME STOCK — stocks which are blue chip or well known and which have a past history of high earnings and dividends, usually stock of low-growth companies.

INFLATION — the loss of purchasing power of the dollar. Shown by an overall general upward price movement of all goods and services.

INFLATION ACCOUNTING — the bookkeeping practice that shows the impact of inflation on corporate assets and profits.

INFLATION HEDGE — an investment which yields a higher return than the rate of inflation.

INHERITANCE TAXES — the state tax on the inheritance received from the estate of the descendant.

INSOLVENCY — the inability to pay one's debts as they mature.

INSTITUTIONS, FINANCIAL — large investing institutions which invest to a degree which greatly affects the securities markets. Includes investment companies, trust departments, insurance companies, and endowments.

INSURANCE DIVIDEND — a payment given to owners of life insurance policies.

INTANGIBLE ASSET — an asset that has no substance or physical body.

INTANGIBLE DRILLING COSTS — the expenses incurred by drilling for oil.

INTERNAL REVENUE CODE — the federal tax code.

INVESTMENT ANALYSIS — a study which results in estimations of the value and probable performance of various investments.

INVESTMENT BANKER — the middleman between the corporation that is issuing new securities and the public.

INVESTMENT BANKING — a business which buys securities from issuers and subsequently sells them to investors.

INVESTMENT COMPANY — an organization which sells its securities to investors and manages the funds in a diversified portfolio of securities.

INVESTMENT COMPANY ACT OF 1940 — federal legislation requiring the registration and regulation of investment companies with the SEC.

INVESTMENT CREDIT — a tax deduction that reduces taxes dollar for dollar.

ISSUED STOCK — authorized stock originally issued to stockholders.

ITEMIZED DEDUCTIONS — a listing of allowed expenses that are subtracted in arriving at taxable income.

## J

JOINT ACCOUNT — an account owned by two or more people.

JOINT TENANCY — a joint ownership of securities which allows the survivor full ownership in the event of the death of the other.

## K

KEOGH BILL — a bill that enables self-employed people to set up tax-saving retirement plans of their own, now referred to as a pension profit sharing plan.

## L

LAND TRUST — title to land held by a trustee in the interest of the beneficiaries of a trust.

LAST IN, FIRST OUT — an accounting term for inventories which price inventories at the most previous costs of the inventory causing the cost of goods sold to be higher and profits to seem lower.

LEASE PURCHASE AGREEMENT — an agreement providing that a portion of a tenant's rent can be applied to the price of purchase.

LEASEBACK — a seller who remains in possession as a tenant after completing the sale and delivering the deed.

LEASEHOLD MORTGAGE — a mortgage on something which is affixed to property which is now owned by the debtor (i.e., building affixed to land which is being leased).

LEGAL LIST STATE — a state which enforces the legal list restriction.

LETTER OF CREDIT — a document issued on behalf of a buyer by a bank on another bank or on itself. It gives the buyer the prestige and the financial backing of the issuing bank.

LETTER STOCK — an unregistered stock, usually issued by a new, small firm to avoid the expense of formal underwriting.

LEVEL PREMIUM INSURANCE — insurance in which the annual premium remains the same throughout the period over which premiums are paid.

LEVERAGE — borrowing money to increase the common stockholders' earnings. For example, if a firm can earn 10% interest on money it borrowed at 5% interest, the extra 5% goes to the common stockholder.

LIABILITY LIMITS — the sum or sums up to which an insurance company protects the insured on a particular policy.

LIEN — a claim on another's property as security against payment of a debt.

LIFE ESTATE — an estate in real or personal property that terminates when the owner dies.

LIFE INSURANCE — insurance providing for payment of a stipulated sum to a designated beneficiary upon the death of the insured.

LIFE INSURANCE TRUST — a trust created by an individual for the benefit of his or her heirs.

LIMITED ORDER — an order in which the customer has set restrictions with respect to price.

LINE OF CREDIT — an agreement between a bank and a customer whereby the bank agrees to lend the customer funds over a future period, up to an agreed maximum amount.

LIQUID — a relative term that applies to ease and speed of converting to cash without excess price concessions.

LIQUID ASSETS — assets that are easily converted into cash.

LIQUIDATION VALUE — the value of a property if the owner were forced to convert it quickly into cash.

LIQUIDITY RATIOS — ratios used during ratio analysis that indicate an organization's ability to meet upcoming financial obligations.

LOAD — fees that must be paid on purchase of mutual funds. There are some no-load funds, but usually they range from 4 to 8.5%.

LONG-TERM CORPORATE BOND — a debt of finance companies, utilities, industrial corporations, and telephone companies.

LONG-TERM DEBT — liabilities that become due more than one year after the signing of the agreement.

LONG-TERM DISABILITY POLICIES — insurance policies that pay covered workers a proportion of their wage or salary when they are disabled.

LONG-TERM LIABILITIES — debts or other obligations that will not be paid for or otherwise discharged within one year or within the normal operating cycle.

LUXURY TAX — a tax imposed on items that are not considered essential for daily living.

# M

MANAGEMENT FEES — fees that investment company managers charge for their management of investment portfolios.

MANIPULATION — an illegal operation that involves buying or selling a security in order to create a false or misleading appearance of active trading or to raise or depress the price to induce purchase or sale by others.

MARGIN — securities: the amount paid by the customer when he or she used a broker's credit to buy a security.

MARGIN CALL — securities: a bank's request for more margin from a borrower when the borrower has securities pledged as loan collateral in a declining market for those securities.

MARGIN REQUIREMENT — the portion of a total purchase price of securities that must be put up in cash.

MARKET MAKER — one who buys and sells a security.

MARKET ORDER — an order to a broker to buy or sell a set number of shares of a stated security at the lowest price possible in the market.

MARKET RISK — a risk associated with the market prices of certain securities. Disruption of the market may cause the security to not be sellable at a fair price when money is needed.

MARKET VALUE — the price of a security or commodity on the daily quotation.

MARKETABLE SECURITIES — short-term investments that can be sold readily in established markets.

MASTER LEASE — an original lease.

MATURITY — a time when the principal of a load or balloon payment of a trust deed is due. A time of completion of the bond indenture.

MONEY MARKET SECURITIES — deposits in financial institutions which are marketable, high-grade, short-term, and used as temporary investments.

MONEY RATE RISK — the risk of changes in interest rates. The prices of long-term bonds and preferred stock may decline due to increased interest rates causing capital loss.

MONTHLY INVESTMENT PLAN (MIP) — a plan which allows investors to buy stock on the New York Stock Exchange through small periodic payments.

MORTGAGE — a written conveyance of title to property, but not possession, to obtain the payment of a debt or the performance of some obligation, under the condition that the conveyance is to be void upon final payment.

MORTGAGE BANKER — a banker who specializes in mortgage financing.

MORTGAGE BONDS — bonds that are backed with specified assets of the company as collateral.

MORTGAGE NOTE — a note that offers a mortgage as proof of an indebtedness and describes the manner in which the mortgage is to be paid.

MUNICIPAL BOND — bonds issued by state and local government which have the advantage of tax-free interest.

MUTUAL FUNDS — a company with no limit on the number of shares it may sell of itself.

# N

NATIONAL ASSOCIATION OF SECURITIES DEALERS (NASD) — an association which oversees the over-the-counter securities business in order to enforce standard procedures and ethics.

NATIONAL ASSOCIATION OF SECURITIES DEALERS AUTOMATED QUOTATIONS (NASDAQ) — an automated information network that provides brokers and dealers with price quotations on securities traded over the counter.

NEGOTIABLE — can transfer ownership.

NET ASSET — the property of a business, corporation, organization, or estate that remains after all obligations have been met.

NET ASSET VALUE — the market value of securities invested in dividends by the number of mutual fund shares outstanding.

NET INCOME — the remains from earnings and profits after all costs, expenses, and allowances for depreciation and probable loss have been deducted.

NET PROFIT — the excess of all revenues over all costs and expenses incurred to obtain the income in a given enterprise during a given period of time.

NET WORTH — represented by the excess of the total assets over the total amounts owed to outside creditors at a given time.

NEW ISSUE — a stock or bond sold by a corporation for the first time.

NON-CALLABLE BOND — a bond that cannot be called by the obliger for redemption or conversion.

NON-DURABLE GOODS — items that have a relatively brief lifetime, e.g., food, clothing.

NORMAL VALUE — the price of a property commanded on the open market.

# O

OBSOLESCENCE — the state of being out-of-date and therefore of little use to society.

ODD-LOT ORDERS — purchases or sales of stock that are not in 100-share units.

OPM — other people's money.

OPTION — 1) real estate: a privilege to buy, sell, receive, or deliver property, given in accordance with terms stated with a consideration for price. 2) securities: an agreement, often for a consideration, to buy or sell a security or commodity within a stipulated time in accordance with the agreement.

ORDINARY LIFE — a type of insurance policy that continues in force throughout the policy holder's lifetime and is payable on his death or when he attains a specified age.

OVER-THE-COUNTER MARKET — a way in which securities are traded without the use of organized stock exchanges. Brokers operate this market through the telephone, computer, and an advertised list.

## P

PAPER PROFIT — an unrealized profit on a security still held. When the security is sold, paper profit becomes a realized profit.

PAR VALUE — the stated or face value of a security.

PENNY STOCKS — low-priced issues that sell at less than one dollar a share.

PENSION PLAN — a method used by a firm or union to pay annuities or pensions to retired and/or disabled employees.

PERIL — the cause of a loss insured against in a policy (e.g., fire, windstorm, explosion).

PERMANENT FINANCING — a long-term mortgage that is amortized over 15, 20, or more years at a fixed rate of interest.

PHYSICAL HAZARD — characteristics of an insurance risk (e.g., material, structural, or operational).

POWER OF ATTORNEY — a written instrument in which one person grants to another the rights of utilization, tenancy, transfer, or disposal of assets owned by the first person as though he himself was exercising these rights (usually acknowledged before a public officer or witness).

PRE-EMPTIVE RIGHTS — the right current stockholders have to buy a pro-rated amount of a new issue of common stock issued by the corporation.

PREFERRED STOCK — in the event that a corporation goes out of business, preferred stock receives dividends and claims on assets preferential to common stock.

PREPAYMENT PENALTY — a penalty placed on a mortgager for paying the mortgage before its due date.

PRESENT VALUE — the discounted value of a certain sum that is due and payable at a specified future date.

PRICE-EARNINGS RATIO — a common stock market value divided by its earnings to be used as a measure of the highness of a stock price.

PROBATE — the right of jurisdiction for hearing and determining questions or issues in matters concerning a will.

PROFIT SHARING — an arrangement whereby employees share in company profits, based on company successes, according to a plan. This compensation is paid in addition to wages.

PROGRESSIVE TAX — an income tax that rises as income increases.

PROMISSORY NOTE — a written promise to pay.

PROSPECTUS — an official document which fully describes a security being issued.

PROXY STATEMENT — written permission a stockholder gives another individual to vote his stock.

PRUDENT MAN RULE — an investment standard. In some states, the law requires that a fiduciary, such as a trustee, invest the fund's money only in a list of securities designated by the state—the so-called legal list.

PURCHASING POWER RISK — the risk of loss of purchasing power of a security through inflation.

PUTS — option contracts that entitle the holder to sell a number of shares of the underlying stock at a stated price on or before a fixed expiration date.

PUTS AND CALLS — options that give the right to buy or sell a fixed amount of certain stock at a specified price within a specified time.

## Q

QUICK RATIO — the ratio between existing liabilities and quick assets, showing a firm's ability to pay off its liabilities rapidly with available funds.

QUIT CLAIM DEED — a document by which one's legal right, title, interest, or claim in a specific property or in an estate held by one's self or others is forever relinquished to another.

## R

REAL INCOME — the sum total of the purchasing power of a national or individual.

RECAPITALIZATION — a corporate process that recapitalizes by exchanging certain securities for others.

RECESSION — a phase of the business cycle that shows a downswing or contraction of the economy.

RECONVEYANCE — transfer of title of property back to a former owner.

REDEEMABLE — returnable to issuing entity.

REFINANCE — to extend existing financing or to acquire new monies, usually done when a mortgage is withdrawn so that a larger one can be placed on the property.

REGISTRAR — an organization which keeps a list of common stockholders and the number of shares they own.

REGULATORY RISK — the risk that a business or security of that business will be impaired due to new laws and regulations or other public policy.

REHYPOTHECATE — to pledge a second time.

REIT — real estate investment trust.

REPURCHASE AGREEMENT — a contractual agreement by an owner to repurchase securities which he or she had sold at a stated price within a stated period of time.

RESCISSION — making void or annulling.

REVENUE BOND — a municipal bond which secured repayment of interest and principal through the revenue earned on a certain project such as toll highways and bridges.

RIDERS — in insurance, forms of special provisions that are not contained in the basic policy contract.

ROUND LOTS — the commonly traded unit on the organized exchanges, usually in blocks of 100 shares.

# S

SAVINGS BOND — a federal obligation which is sold either on a discount basis to compound to par or at par to pay semi-annual interest.

SECOND LIEN — a lien that ranks after the first lien and is to be fulfilled next.

SECURED DEBT — any debt for which some form of acceptable collateral has been pledged.

SECURITIES AND EXCHANGE COMMISSION (SEC) — the federal agency that oversees and regulates the securities business and the various federal security laws.

SELF-INSURANCE — a system whereby a firm or individual, by setting aside an amount of money, provides for the occurrence of any losses that could ordinarily be covered under an insurance program.

SELLERS' MARKET — a market in which demand is greater than supply, resulting in sellers setting the prices and terms of sale. It is a market characterized by rising or high prices.

SELLER'S OPTION — a special transaction on an exchange whereby the seller holding the option can deliver the stocks or bonds at any time within a specified period, ranging from not less than six business days to not more than 60 days.

SELLER'S SEVEN SALE — an agreed-upon delay of seven or more days for the delivery of a security.

SENIOR SECURITIES — the securities which have a higher claim to the assets of a company upon liquidation than common stock—usually bonds and preferred stock.

SETTLEMENT DAY — the deadline by which a purchaser of stock must pay for what has been bought and the seller must deliver the certificates for the securities that have been sold.

SHORT SALE — selling securities you do not own in anticipation of a decline in the price. The shares are borrowed from a broker and later bought back and repaid to the broker.

SHORT SELLING — selling a stock and purchasing it at a lower price to receive a profit.

SINKING FUND — a fund of a corporation which is paid into periodically in order to secure the subsequent payments of bond or preferred stock issues.

SOFT MONEY — paper currency as contrasted with coinage (hard money).

SPECULATION — owning or trading unstable securities hoping for capital gains or large income. The investor is willing to take large amounts of risk.

STOCK — the legal capital of a corporation divided into shares.

STOCK DIVIDEND — a portion of the net earnings of a corporation, payable (in shares or fractional shares of designated stock of a given corporation) to the stockholders of record of the corporation.

STOCK SPLIT — a process by which a corporation increases the number of shares by dividing its existing shares. Reduces the price per share of the stock by diluting the equity per share.

STOP ORDER — an order to buy at a price above or to sell at a price below the current market. Stop-buy orders are generally used to limit loss or to protect unrealized profits on a short sale.

STRAIGHT-LINE DEPRECIATION — the simplest method of depreciation.

STREET NAME — describing a stock certificate in the name of a broker who trades in securities and is a member of an exchange. This stock is never considered a part of the broker's personal wealth.

SUBLEASE — the letting of premises to a third party with the original tenant retaining an interest in the property.

SURRENDER VALUE — designating the amount of the total life insurance in force that will be paid to the policy holder, after a certain stipulated number of premiums have been paid, if the policy holder elects to surrender the policy and receive such proportionate part.

# T

TAX CREDIT — a direct reduction in tax liability, usually granted to encourage a particular action or to provide tax relief for certain classes of taxpayers.

TAX EXEMPTION — a right, secured by law, permitting freedom from a charge of taxes (e.g., on income that constitutes primary support of a child).

TAX SHELTER — a means of legal avoidance of paying a portion of one's income taxes by careful interpretation of tax regulations and adjustments of one's finances to take advantage of IRS rulings.

TAXABLE INCOME — the amount of income remaining after all permitted deductions and exemptions have been subtracted.

TENANCY BY THE ENTIRETY — an estate jointly owned by a husband and wife. The survivor receives the total estate. This agreement cannot be broken without the consent of both spouses.

TENANCY IN COMMON — ownership of property by two or more persons, each holding a separate interest. No right of survivorship exists.

TERM POLICY — usually a fire or casualty policy written for more than one year; not to be confused with term life insurance.

TESTAMENTARY TRUST — a trust established through a will. The trustee is named in the will to receive designated property from the executor of an estate and to hold it in trust for the benefit of named beneficiaries.

THIN MARKET — a market in which there are few buy-and-sell offers.

TIME DEPOSIT (open account) — funds deposited under agreement that bear interest from the date of deposit, although the agreement usually requires that such funds remain on deposit for at least 30 days. The agreement stipulates a fixed maturity date or number of days after which payment will be made, or it is stipulated that payment will be made after a given period following notice by the depositor of intention to withdraw.

TIME-SHARING PRIORITY — a ranking within the group of tasks associated with a single user, used to determine their precedence for the allocation of system resources.

TREASURY BILL — a U.S. Government short-term security, sold to the public each week.

TREASURY CERTIFICATES — U.S. Government short-term securities, sold to the public and maturing in one year.

TREASURY NOTE — a U.S. Government long-term security, sold to the public and maturing in one to five years.

TREASURY STOCK — the title to previously issued stock of a corporation that has been reacquired by that corporation by purchase, gift, donation, inheritance, or other means.

TRUSTEE — a person to whom the title to property has been conveyed for the benefit of another.

# U

UMBRELLA LIABILITY — a form of insurance protection against losses in excess of amounts covered by other liability insurance policies. It also protects the insured in many situations that are not covered by the usual liability policies. Such insurance is usually written for sums in the $1 million range for professionals, executives, and businessmen who may be liable to malpractice suits and other large liability claims.

UNINSURED MOTORIST PROTECTION — a form of insurance that covers the policy holder and members of his or her family in the event of injury by a hit-and-run motorist or by a driver who carries no liability insurance, assuming that the other driver is at fault.

UNIT TRUST — a British term for mutual investment; a mutual fund.

UNSECURED DEBT — a debt for which no collateral has been pledged.

## V

VARIABLE ANNUITY — an annuity contract providing lifetime retirement payments that vary in amount with the results of investment in a separate account portfolio.

## W

WAGE FREEZE — a limit on salary increases, usually imposed by a government.

## Y

YIELD TO MATURITY — the rate of return on an investment when it is retained until maturity, given as a percentage.

## Z

ZERO COUPON BOND — redeemed at the full amount at maturity, a security sold at a deep discount from its face value.

# AFTERWORD

Remember, the information provided in this book is only a reference point. Your individual needs may vary from what has been discussed. To safeguard your millionaire future, the wisest course of action is to consult a professional in the areas of your concerns.

For all of you who have read this book and would like to discuss these ideas further, I am available to help you in any way I can. I invite you to write to me at

P.O. Box 661540
Sacramento, California 95825

or call (916) 973-8181. I look forward to hearing from you.

I hope you have enjoyed reading this book. I certainly enjoyed writing it. In fact, I enjoyed writing it so much, I am working on its sequel: *The Aspiring Millionaire, Part II.*

And one more reminder Good luck! You, and you alone, will determine your destiny!

# The Aspiring Millionaire Accessory Kit

181

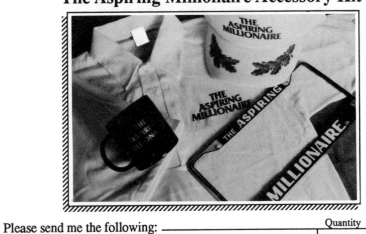

Please send me the following:

|  | Quantity | Total |
|---|---|---|
| **ASPIRING MILLIONAIRE POLO SHIRT** $24.95<br>In comfortable 50/50 cotton / polyester blend. Available in white only with exclusive ASPIRING MILLIONAIRE logo in blue. Men's sizes S / M / L (circle one) | | |
| **ASPIRING MILLIONAIRE CAP** $8.95<br>Distinctively embroidered with gold leaves on visor with ASPIRING MILLIONAIRE logo in blue. In durable white nylon fabric; adjustable to fit all. | | |
| **ASPIRING MILLIONAIRE COFFEE MUG** $7.95<br>The look of fine ceramic. Black finish with gold logo. Chip proof and break resistant. Beautiful. | | |
| **ASPIRING MILLIONAIRE LICENSE FRAME** $14.95<br>A truly handsome touch to your automobile. The look of elegant brass with ASPIRING MILLIONAIRE logo set in white against black background. (order two for $24.95) | | |
| **ASPIRING MILLIONAIRE TRAINING TAPES** (not shown) $29.95 set of tapes<br>Listen while you drive or just relax while the author himself reviews a structured learning course on acquiring wealth and a winning attitude. Learn what it takes to make the right decisions. Order this complete set of tapes and experience a more successful financial future. | | |
| **ASPIRING MILLIONAIRE CLUB** $3.00 year<br>Receive information through out the year on investment ideas and valuable business tips. Belong to this exclusive group of serious acheivers. | | Sub Total |
| Check one: ☐ Check | | |
| **Allow six weeks for delivery -** postage and shipping fee is $1.00 per item. ☐ Money Order | | Postage & Shipping Total |
| NAME_____ | | |
| ADDRESS_____ | | Grand Total |
| CITY_____STATE_____ZIP_____ | | |

Make check payable to: **Aspiring Millionaires Publishing House**
P.O. Box 661540 - A, Sacramento, CA 95825

*Thank You!*

# References on materials used:

1. Rosenberg, Jerry M. Dictionary of Business and Management, 2nd Ed. 1983

2. G. & C. Merriam Company. Webster's New Collegiate Dictionary, 1981

# A PROFITABLE OPPORTUNITY

As an individual or organization, you are probably interested in saving and/or making money. Many people just like you have made hundreds of thousands of dollars selling popular books This is possible when you buy at wholesale level, mark them up, and sell them at retail prices.

This book, THE ASPIRING MILLIONAIRE, is ideal for this profit-making venture. It is also perfect for large (and small) financial institutions as a promotional tool for clients and a training manual for your staff.

Simply complete the attached coupon, and send with a check or money order made payable to: ASPIRING MILLIONAIRES PUBLISHING HOUSE.

---

### ASPIRING MILLIONAIRES PUBLISHING HOUSE
#### P.O. Box 661540
#### Sacramento, CA 95825

| Quantity | $ per Book | x | Quantity Chosen | = | Enclosed Amount |
|---|---|---|---|---|---|
| 1 – 5 | $14.95 | x | _____ | = | $_____ |
| 5 – 10 | $12.95 | x | _____ | = | $_____ |
| 10 – 50 | $10.95 | x | _____ | = | $_____ |
| 50 – 100 | $ 9.95 | x | _____ | = | $_____ |
| 100 – 500 | $ 8.95 | x | _____ | = | $_____ |
| 500 and more | $ 7.95 | x | _____ | = | $_____ |

Please send me _____ copies of THE ASPIRING MILLIONAIRE. I have enclosed $_____ for this order. I understand it will take 4 to 6 weeks for delivery.

Cover price includes postage and handling. No cash, credit cards, or CODs. Prices are subject to change without notice.